T0065155

WHAT GOD SAID

DR. CHRIS OKEKE

authorHOUSE

AuthorHouse™
1663 Liberty Drive
Bloomington, IN 47403
www.authorhouse.com
Phone: 833-262-8899

Published by AuthorHouse 07/29/2020

ISBN: 978-1-7283-6824-5 (sc)
ISBN: 978-1-7283-6933-4 (e)

Print information available on the last page.

DEDICATION

TO MY ONLY SAVIOR
JESUS CHRIST

MY FRIEND, WIFE, BETTER HALF MRS HELEN OKEKE WHO HAS SOLIDLY STOOD WITH ME AS WE DAILY BEEN REFINED BY THE FIRE OF GOD IN OTHER TO DO WHAT GOD SAID. IN YOU I SEE THE WOMAN OF GOD. MAY THE LORD CONTINUE TO INCREASE HIS WISDOM AND ANOINTING IN YOU, IN THE NAME OF JESUS CHRIST.

TO OUR CHILDREN, GIFT AND FAVOUR OKEKE. I PRAY THAT GOD WILL GIVE YOU DOUBLE POTIONS OF THE ANOINTING TO STAND FOR HIM IN YOUR GENERATION, IN THE JESUS CHRIST, AMEN.

CONTENTS

INTRODUCTION

We live in a time when God wants all His followers to act on what He said in His word, the Bible. Acting on what God said is a sure evidence of our love for Him. Jesus said "If you love Me, keep My commandments" John 14:15.

God sees your love for Him by your obedience to what He said to you. God spoke generally spoke to the church. He also spoke specifically to us you and me on some personal issues. Yes, He spoke to you at some point since you come to know Him as your personal Lord and savior. He still speaks to you now and will continue to speak until your last breath on this side of eternity. The question is, what did you do with what He said to you? The ultimate answer to this obvious question rests on your willingness to do what He said. He has already equipped you to focus on and carryout His commandments, as written in the Bible. He indwells you by His Spirit through which He will accomplish His purpose for which He kept you alive.

Another obvious question is, are you available for Him? You cannot do what He said if you are not available. Available means to be ready at someone's disposal, or someone's use. Are you available for God? I will discuss availability as we go on this discussion.

This book case studies those who had evidently served the Lord before us, Abraham, Isiah, Noah, and so on. They can be seen as successful servants of God. As we embark on this exploration experience, we are to learn how they responded to what God said to them, and what they did with it that catapulted them to the position of been known as "Obedient men and women of God." We will be able to learn some fundamental principles of obedience that will help us live by faith for God alone. These principle, as we learn, will bring us to the level of acceptance before the Lord. More so to be more effective at serving Him.

This season of our existence requires an urgent attention to what God said in His word. Our reaction to what He said in His word is of paramount importance to God. It is absolutely important to take God seriously by doing what He said.

As days go by, so our lives draws closer to eternity in heaven. What is more important for us is to act in the most practical ways about what God said. The earlier we engage in this assignment in the most meaningful ways, the better for us to be prepared for the rewards that follow obedience. Beloved follow as the Holy Spirit leads. Amen.

Rev. Dr Chris. N. Okeke.
August 14th 2019.

CHAPTER 1

Challenging Times.

We are living in a challenging times, challenging because the second coming of Jesus Christ is right here. Jesus Christ revealed to his disciples about these times as a sign of the "end of the age" and more so, His coming back to the earth. (Lk 24). There will be more unpredictable periods of challenges ahead; in other words, more trying times will show up until the final day when Jesus Christ will appear. The foretold signs preceding His coming continue to surface and culminate. The day is not far when the trumpet will be blown, announcing the end of the world, and that is why we should strive to do what God said.

Presently, we are witnesses of the persecution and hatred meted to Christians all over the world. Our faith is challenged daily, "But know this, that in the last days [a]perilous times will come: For men will be lovers of themselves, lovers of money, boasters, proud, blasphemers, disobedient to parents, unthankful, unholy, unloving, unforgiving, slanderers, without self-control, brutal, despisers of good, traitors, headstrong, haughty, lovers of pleasure rather than lovers of God, having a form of godliness but denying its power. And from such people turn away! For of this sort are those who creep into households and make captives of gullible women loaded down with sins, led away by various lusts, always learning and never able to come to the knowledge of the truth." 2 Timothy 3:1-7. These issues are what we all are witnessing in our community today.

These challenging times affects the church all over the world. At some point in lives, the believers of Jesus Christ in different nations had witnessed some kind of persecution, which included killing, burning of places of worship, imprisonments and other forms of persecutions. There are more false prophets everywhere than the church had ever seen before. More people are deceived than are converted to faith in Jesus Christ. Some governments of these nations delved into altering the systems of worship and outline some unbiblical terminology meant to be a teaching guide, preachers are expected to follow these guidelines in presenting their sermons to the congregation. These authorities threatened that anyone who violates these principles will end up in jail, usually long jail terms. In fact, an in-depth investigation focusing on global Christian persecution gave an alarming rate by which Christians are killed for their faith in Jesus Christ. Open door USA, an independent organization whose objectives are to monitor Christians persecuting nations and find a way to stop it, reported that eleven Christians are massacred daily in 50 major countries in the watch list. In some of these countries, being a Christian is equal to warranting a death sentence. Can you imagine what our persecuted brethren are experiencing in a daily basis? Our churches are besieged and attacked by other faiths while the governments of these nations turn their attentions to other less important matters. All that the church is presently going through had already been predicted; it is sign of the end. Jesus wants us to watch out so as not to be taken unawares. Our intimate relationship with Him is the most significant concern at this time of our life. Also, we are to work to fulfill our ministers before the trumpet sounds.

A while ago, a discussion made me ponder why God set up the churches, is it for determination of true believers? But then, who are the true believers? .The theological answers to this question are those who radically obey what God said in the Bible. Beloved, it is time to obey What God said! For that is the only way to please Him. Yes, the situation of the church calls for total unadulterated Obedience to what God said. As already discussed above, there is an increase in the persecution of the Churches around the world. Jesus speaking to His disciples said, "ember the word that I said to you, 'A servant is not greater than his master.' If they persecuted Me, they will also persecute you. If they kept My word, they will keep yours also" John15:20

These situations also affect the preaching of the word of God; many preachers preach what the people want to hear, not what God said is saying in His word. Their sermons are watered down in other to maintain the numerical value of the congregation. The words preached have no spiritual intonation. As a result, our churches are filled with people with Nicodemus syndrome, which talks of the Knowledge of the law and not the personal relationship with Jesus Christ.

Acting on what God said has many rewards, both spiritual and physical:

1. It ushers in the blessings of God on you and your family.
2. God sees you as His child (because now you have a personal relationship with His son Jesus Christ).
3. It is the only way to show your love for God.
4. As a result of the blessings of God on you, unbelievers are attracted to follow Jesus.
5. As a result of obedience, the church becomes powerful, more disciples made. Matthew 24:13
6. It strengthens the belief in God and gives strong foundation to the faithful worshippers.
7. God trusts you and reveals things to you. (Abraham, Elijah, Elisha, Moses, etc.).

God is still speaking even now.

God spoke in the past through various means. He spoke to every seen and unseen element; they all responded to His voice and obeyed what He said. God said, Let there be light, and there was light. God also said, "Let the waters under the heaven be gathered together unto one place and let the dry land appear, and it was so. God called the dry land Earth, and the gathering of waters "He called the seas." Take a quick spiritual observation yourself, look outside your house, observe the world around you; what you see would never be if it was not for God's decree.

The changing directions of winds, the rustling of leaves, the rumbles of seas, what you see, hear and experience operates under God's commands. Every creation reacts directly to God's commandments—they live, function and react according to the voice of God. God wants man to do what He said in the Bible. The Bible reveals to us the mind of God, and how to live in it. It controls the universe we dwell in.

Every creation known and unknown hears the voice of God and react to what they heard. God spoke to his creations, specifically to the individuals. You are one of the people God spoke to in on a personal way, and. We are to obey what He said. As you obey, the Holy Spirit releases the joy that follows obedience. The Scripture says, if you obey, you will eat the fruit of the land. The joy of the Lord comes when His children obey His commandments.

"What God said" is written specifically for humanity. He requires a practical response from us by putting what He said into practice. Yes, not only does He want you to hear but also to live by it daily. God knows our frame and that we cannot perfectly obey Him, which is why He indwelled us by His Holy Spirit to help us live in obedience to His word. God is looking for those obedient children who He will trust to be in charge of His inheritance. God's inheritance is His people, you and I included. "For God so loved the world that He gave His only begotten Son, that whoever believes in Him should not perish but have everlasting life." Jn 3:16. Are you going to be one of the people God will trust? The choice is yours. God is waiting for you to say yes. Your yes means that you will be living in obedience to whatever He says in His word. His word is there for us to respond to. He is waiting for you to make a decision to obey His word.

Facts about the word of God.

The word of God is God.

Every single word of God, as written in the Bible, is meant to be:

- Heard by us.
- Accepted by us.
- Obeyed by us. (That is put it into action or let it rule every action).

It is written for our benefits.

The word of God reveals who God is.

The word of God reveals His personality (Love, compassion, mercy, Grace). The word of God reveals His omnipotent character. He gives you understanding of His word.

He reveals to you His ultimate intention for the man (you).

It becomes, therefore, as a matter of urgency to adhere to the things that God said to us and start following the specific direction He gave. Not only hearing and believing, but also to act on it and live by it daily. 2nd Timothy Says,

"All Scripture is given by inspiration of God, and is profitable for doctrine, for reproof, for correction, for instruction in righteousness, that the man of God may be complete, thoroughly equipped for every good work." 2 Timothy 3:16-17

God had been in existence before the time began. He has no beginning and no end. He existed from generation to generation, every generation experienced His awesome presence and personality.

- They experience His love.
- They experience His Mercy.
- They experience His compassion.

- They experience His Grace.
- They experience His presence.
- They have hope in Him for eternal life.

The God of the Old Testament is the same God of the New Testament. What He did in the past He is still doing it today, in your life and as well as mine. The Scripture says, "God is the same yesterday, today and forever."

God is all in all

God allows adequate wrath for those who disobey His commandments. He spoke all things into existence. The modern scientists and wisdom of men could not understand the concept of creation and the nature of God. They were not able to bring to a conclusion the fact that God created the world and all things seen and unseen. To them, the world came into existence by chance. The most established philosophers of our time also could not establish how God began or the number of years He had been in existence or who He is. The Scripture clearly informed us that nobody has ever seen God at any time in the history of the world. But the Scripture said that Jesus Christ is God, John 1:1. God came into the world in the person of Jesus and became flesh to save man from sins. Jesus said, "My father and I are one." He indwells those who receive Him as Lord and savior by His Spirit. In the plain term, God lives in us, and we are God carriers; that is why each individual is a unique being. Yes, you are specially made and preserved for eternity. You are the elect of God.

Jesus speaking to His disciples said, "I am the way, the truth, and the life. No one comes to the Father except through Me" Jn 14:6

Jesus is everything we need in life. He is everywhere at the same time, in the sea, ocean, sky, in the womb He is basically everywhere, that is why Jonah can call on Him in the belly of a fish from the depths of the sea, and He answered Jonah and delivered Him from the near-death situation.

The same God who delivered Jonah from the belly of a fish will deliver you from whatever afflictions you are presently going through. He is God Himself, a miracle worker whose existence is beyond human perception. He was neither born nor made or created. He spoke to create things; he spoke to them before and after creation., He spoke to humanity from generation to generation. Everything responds positively to the sound of his name. God has said something about you, and is still speaking to you. Did you respond?

God spoke specifically to those who come to Him through Jesus Christ. He also spoke to you and me through various levels of afflictions we experience. The main purpose of this book is to explore through case studies of people to whom who God has said something and how they reacted to what He said, and what they did with what He said. Whatever God said to you needed a response. He expects you to act on it.

I believe that when we act on what God said and apply it to our lives daily, the totality of our lives will change to His glory. Have you taken time out to think of what God said to you? First, God spoke to humanity to believe on the Lord Jesus Christ, you and your family, and you shall be saved. (Act 16:31).

When you believe and confess Jesus Christ as Lord and savior, the following principles will be evident in your life:

1. You will have eternal life in Jesus Christ.
2. You will have knowledge of God through His son Jesus Christ.
3. You will have a personal and intimate relationship with Him.
4. You will be indwelled by His Spirit.
5. You will have the blessings that come with obedience. (Deuteronomy 28)
6. You will have the peace of God in you and your family.
7. God will trust you because of your obedience to His word. John 14:15
8. God will bless you and make you a blessing.
9. Peace of God will surround you and your family.

10. You will experience God's love in a daily basis.
11. God will see you as His child. John 1:12.
12. God will promote you spiritually, and give you reasons to celebrate.

You are made in His image.

Beloved, you are made in the image of God. (Genesis 1:26) Image can be described as something that looks like the original, and also has unique some characteristics. In photography, after you take a picture, the first production of the picture is the image; this shows all the images of the pictures taken and not the original. The scripture says that God is a Spirit; those who worship Him must worship Him in spirit and in truth. Being in accord with reality and facts is what defines truth, and the biggest reality is that every individual is a unique person. He indwells us by His Spirit. He lives and speaks to us daily. He shapes us spiritually in His image. He takes care of us at all times.

His ultimate desire at all times is for us to be just like Him. Jesus said, "Therefore you shall be perfect, just as your Father in heaven is perfect" Matthew 5:48.

Every good parent wants his children to look and act like him, so as our God. He wants us to be like Him, to act and do what He does, have compassion and love one another as He loved us. Jesus Christ said, "Because it is written, 'Be holy, for I am holy.'" 1 Peter 1:16.

As already discussed, God has no shape or form. The scripture says that God is a Spirit and, therefore, exists without a body. But He can be what He wants to be so He became a man and lived among us. He incarnated Himself in other form to fulfill His purpose for man, His name is Jesus Christ. John 1:14 says, "And the Word became flesh and dwelt among us, and we beheld His glory, the glory as of the only begotten of the Father, full of grace and truth." in the same manner John bared witness of Him and cried saying, "This was He of whom I said, 'He who comes after me is preferred before me, for He was before me.'" John 1:15. He indwells us by His Spirit. Therefore, we are supposed to possess some special qualities as a result of His presence in us.

God said something to Himself (God the Father, God the Son, God the Holy Spirit). "Let Us make man in Our image, according to Our likeness; let them have dominion over the fish of the sea, over the birds of the air, and over the cattle, over all the earth and over every creeping thing that creeps on the earth." Genesis 1:26.

You are loaded with Godhead, (Father, Son, and Holy Spirit). You are enveloped with His love, mercy and power. It was because of His love for us that He decided to save us from our sins and gave us eternal life-- you are a special child in God's eyes. As you believed and confessed Jesus Christ as Lord and savior, God releases His potentials inside of you, so you can be a better child of God by keeping His commandments.

Your belief and trust will lead you into greater knowledge and a balanced faith in Him. His power is available to tap on, at this moment if you accept His offer of love in the person of Jesus Christ. You know, God never holds back His potential and releases power for you to use in the time of need. Especially if you share the gospel to others, He speaks through you to the unbelievers --yes, you are God's voice. If you acknowledge this revelation, then it becomes obvious that your voice will never again be used to swear, lie, curse or any other vulgar words.

The Grace of God is upon you, and your voice is sanctified to minister God's mercies to people that are in need. Apostle Peter spoke in line to this, and said to a lame man, "In the name of Jesus Christ of Nazareth rise up and walk, the lame or crippled man rose and walked; You have the same quality as Peter and other apostles. You can pray in the name of Jesus Christ, and God will respond immediately, all the afflictions or the problem hear the name of God and bow.

Believe in the Lord Jesus Christ + Faith in His Word, then command any situation that is standing contrary to you in the name of Jesus Christ. Regardless of how difficult your situation is, take the name of Jesus Christ and see how your afflictions cease to exist. The scripture said, "That at the name of Jesus every knee should bow, of those in heaven, and of those on earth, and of those under the earth." (Philippians 2:10)

Note beloved, everything that God created consists of the word of God. This is because God spoke them into existence. The word of God can bring a change to everything and to anything.

God said, "Let there be light, and there was light". This means that the word of God has all the power to create. "For the word of God is living and powerful, and sharper than any two-edged sword, piercing even to the division of soul and spirit, and of joints and marrow, and is a discerner of the thoughts and intents of the heart." Hebrews 4:12

It is absolutely important to go back to the Bible and study it and believe what He said to us and act on it. Acting on what He said is healthy living. In it, you find solutions to life's problems. Living by what God said is the highest form of spiritual connection to Him. It also increases our faith to accomplish great things, which ordinarily cannot be accomplished. It will change your situation or anyone you are ministering to. I used to suffer from Malaria and fever every month, but it all came to an end when I became the child of God by inviting Jesus Christ in my life as Lord and savior. I read and apply the word of God in my life with as much grace that I was given. With my little faith in the Lord Jesus Christ, the yearly sickness of malaria and Fever left me to this day. To the glory of God, all the complaints of headache and feverish conditions were gone, I began to enjoy good healthy lifestyle. My wife Helen also had the same testimony of divine healing as a result of her faith in the Lord Jesus Christ. The power of God is still available today. God is always standing to back up His word with signs and wonders.

Every answer we need about creation and all things can be found in the Bible, the word of God. God intelligently placed all things where they are for a reason and, to fulfill His purposes. Think of the oceans, the rivers, the ground we walk on, the trees of the bush, the house we live in, the rain, the sun, the hills, the valleys, all perform God's purposes. The word of God says, " The earth is the Lord's, and all its fullness, The world and those who dwell therein." Psalms 24:1 As already said, God designed all things to perform certain functions. In essence, where you are right now is where God intended you to be. Where you live is where God wants you to live. Wherever you are, God expects you to represent Him. He anointed you to be His ambassador 2 Corinthians 5:20 says, "Now then, we are ambassadors for Christ, as though God were pleading through us: we implore you on Christ's behalf, be reconciled to God." God wants total unadulterated obedience to Him in His words. As you step out to do His will, He empowers you so you can achieve the desired goal.

Every creature hears the word of God and respond to the commands given. They hear the name of Jesus and immediately responds to what He said. Every created things responds when you speak in the name of Jesus Christ. Heavens stand at attention, waiting for instruction or direction on what to do when you call the name of Jesus Christ. The Scripture says that, "That at the name of Jesus every knee should bow, of those in heaven, and of those on earth, and of those under the earth, 11 and that every tongue should confess that Jesus Christ is Lord, to the glory of God the Father." Philippians 2:10-11

When the word is spoken from a repentant heart, God hears immediately and responds to the request made. Your own words spoken ordinarily has no power to change things. The word of God has the authority and power to accomplish things. The word of God is alive and living. "In the beginning was the Word, and the Word was with God, and the Word was God." John 1:1 The more you access His word, the more your faith grows in Him. Your confession of faith in the Lord Jesus Christ is the express path to receive your needs. Obedience to the word of God is all you need to deal with issues that are contrary to your well-being. Obedience automatically ushers in abundant blessings. You can change anything and every situation by the word of God. For in the name of Jesus Christ, you have access to all you want to accomplish. You and I can have access to our needs through faith in His name.

The book of numbers chapter 16 informs us of how Moses commanded the earthquake to consume his enemies, the earth responded when it heard the word of God from the man of God. Instantly, an earthquake occurred and all those troubling Moses died through the earthquake. This was a story of Koran, Dothan, Abiram, and 250 other Israelites representing the congregation of the Israelite who rebelled against Moses and Aaron. Moses said, "By this, you shall know that the Lord has sent me to do all these works, for I have not done them of my own will." verse 29. You have a divine calling. God called you by Jesus Christ, you have qualities of Him who called. He gave you His name, which changes every situation. You have to access His name in every situation of concerns.

If you speak to anything in the name of Jesus, that particular thing has no option but to concur and do all you asked. The ground did not hear Moses name; it heard the voice of God and respond to what was demanded. The people rebelled against Moses the man of God, as a result of their action, instant judgement was pronounced on them, causing an earthquake to destroy the ring leaders and their families.

We are positioned to exercise God's power in your life and bring everything that is troubling you under control. When you speak from the voice of faith in the name of Jesus Christ, every knee bows and every tongue confesses that Jesus Christ is Lord. God always backs up His word to bring you closer to the purpose for which He spoke to you. You are appointed to do what you are presently doing for the kingdom of God. God increases your faith in Him if you faithfully do what He asked you to do. He will equip you with His power and anointing so that you can be effective in doing the work of God as you help more people get closer to the glory of God. You are in Covenant with God. You are protected and covered by the blood of Jesus. The Bible declares that you are in covenant with Him through His blood. The book of mark recorded "Then He took the cup, and when He had given thanks He gave it to them, and they all drank from it. And He said to them, "This is My blood of the [a]new covenant, which is shed for many." Mark 14:23-24 A covenant is a type of agreement, undertaking, commitment, or establishing a relationship between two parties. You are in a covenant relationship with Jesus Christ. If you confess Jesus as your Lord and savior, then you have entered into a covenant with Him through His shed blood.

The Holy Spirit reveals in your spirit that you are not alone; I do believe that you have already claimed this truth. You are endowed with His presence and His power that surpasses every existing power in the universe. You are not whom you used to be-- you are a Spirit, you are powerful, you are God's child with God's nature. You are in the world and not part of the world-- you are a citizen of heaven. The Scripture says, "because He who is in you is greater than he who is in the world." 1 John 4:4 .You see, beloved, because God is God by Himself; He never change or alters in His dealings with us, and keeps each of His promise to us. As a believer of Jesus Christ, with His blessings upon you, you have the power greater than every other power put together. As already mentioned, we are in His blood covenant. It was shedding of this blood that we have been saved. This covenant points to our salvation, our deliverance from sacrifices of any nature. His blood is the one-time sacrifice for humanity shed on the cross of Calvary. For us, our responsibility is to keep the terms of the blood covenant. It is done by following the Lord's footsteps and keep doing what God said. Failure to do what He commanded is sinful. In one way or the other, we have all sinned and disobeyed God in many categories of life. He loves us and still wants us to be saved and have eternal life in Him.

The Bible declares that "If we confess our sins, He is faithful and just to forgive us our sins and to cleanse us from all unrighteousness." 1 John 1:9. This is the good news that we can still be forgiven if we accidentally sinned.

God reassures us that we are covered and protected under the terms of His covenant with us. The key term of the covenant is the Cross. Those who have invited Jesus Christ as Lord and savior, carry the cross day in day out by their walks for the Lord. Most of them face daily persecution, and some are inhumanly treated by different nations of the world.

God also commanded all his creation concerning His children; Saying, "Do not touch My anointed ones, And do My prophets no harm." Psalm 105:15. This commandment is directed to everything that walks against you, including sickness and other kinds of afflictions. God Himself is our sanctuary, protecting us from calamities and distress through His sacredness. God's protection keep us safe from our enemies, no matter what your circumstances are.

God's word also holds the rivers and the oceans in one place. The God who holds up the sky and stars in its place, also holds the key to everything unknown and known. Everything seen and unseen are kept by the word of His power. As already discussed, God's commanded the animals in the bush, and other creatures to submit to man. God said, "Saying, "Do not touch My anointed ones, And do My prophets no harm." Psalm 105:15. God's commandments kept them away from harming us. They all heard the word of God and obeyed it. Disobedience to God's commandment is sin, it is disrespectful or noncompliance.

God spoke precisely to the first man, Adam, and his wife Eve. Yes, God spoke in general to them and He also said something specifics to them. "See, I have given you every herb that yields seed which is on the face of all the earth, and every tree whose fruit yields seed; to you it shall be for food." Gen. 1:29.

The Bible contains the general instructions that God gave to His people of Israel. On one occasion, God said to Moses "Speak to all the congregation of the children of Israel, and say to them: 'You shall be holy, for I the Lord your God am holy." Leviticus 19:1-2. God spoke in general terms to other prophets, giving them instructions either for the individual or the generality of the people. Whenever there are urgent needs to protect His children, or to get His their attention, or to seek Him on important issues, He then speak on general terms. He expects them to obey and follow through to what He said without any form of refusal. Whatever God says to you is good and blessings if you do as He said. If God determines that you are willing to obey, He now gives you step by step instructions on how are you are going to be successful in fulfilling what He said. When Moses kept God's instructions to bring the children of Israel from bondage in Egypt, He gave him step by step specific instructions, which led to the total emancipation of the federation of the Israelites. Beloved God will walk with you if you obey and recognize Him as the only God and put Him first in your life.

As already mentioned, whatever God said to us needs to be followed through and get it accomplished. Failure to do what God said accounts to our disobedience. It is carelessness and disrespect to Him. Many times God has said some specific things to me, which I out of carelessness failed to do. I remember some time ago through the inner witness of the Holy Spirit, He instructed me to go and share the gospel message of salvation to a man of about 77 years. This gentleman used to fast and pray, and he attended church and morning prayers at a scheduled time. But he did not know Jesus Christ as personal Lord and savior. Later he got sick, it was then that I had the Holy Spirit prompting me to travel to where this man lives and share the message of salvation with him. I kept postponing it until the man died. I was so troubled in my spirit that I had to go back to the Holy Spirit to ask for forgiveness for my nonchalant behavior and neglect. I learnt a big lesson from this incident.

I lived with this, and blaming myself until I felt loved and forgiveness for this incident. We are to pay attention to the inner witness of the Spirit to know when we receive specific instructions for something to be done. I have also obeyed some specific instructions from God, and the obedience led to open up to me and used me helped me to lead people to Him through salvation message.

God wants our attention.

God woes us constantly to get our attention, but the worldly cares and our personal goals have impeded our spiritual growth. Our spiritual growth is far more important than our personal needs. For when we are connected to God through His only begotten son Jesus Christ. He will then meet our needs one by one. The book of Matthew put it this way, "Seek first the kingdom of God and His righteousness and all these things shall be added to you." Matthew 6:33.

To get God's attention,

1. Seek Him through His son Jesus Christ.
2. Read and study the Bible everyday

3. Follow His teaching.
4. Reach out to other people who have not known Him with the gospel.
5. Be determined to flee from those habits which hinder your spiritual growth.
6. Attend the fellowship of believers as much as you can.
7. Rely on the Holy Spirit alone for directions instead of relying on yourself alone.
8. Obey God in all things, including supporting your congregation with your tithe and giving and other ministries that promote growth of the kingdom of God. Such as radio and other evangelical arms of the Church.

It is our responsibility to choose the part of obedience. We are in the season of applying what God said to us in our daily orientations. We have read the Bible long enough to understand to some extent that God desires obedience. The simple truth remains that if we fail to act on what God said, it shows that we do not love Him. Secondly, it is a part way to our spiritual down grade. Our conversations and action may seem to gravitate towards worldly ideology. When this happens it leads you into spiritual struggle trying to stand for the Lord-- this is seen as "Back sliding." Beloved you and I do not want our faith to be downgraded. Satan's main job is to make sure that we fail spiritually if he fails to achieve this, then he will find other ways to make sure that we disobey God in some way. That is why we should depend totally, and unshakably to Jesus Christ. You do not want to leave yourself an open ground for the enemy to trample on and change your perspective about Jesus Christ. You have the resources needed to withstand the attacks of the enemy Jesus is your resource. As already stated, God started to talk to humanity through Adam and Eve and is still speaking to us. As we explore this episode on what God said to you, we want to look at what God said to Adam and subsequent prophets and other faithful who have lived and have gone home to the Lord. From this Biblical examples we will learn how to approach and embark on all that God had said. Let us consider some of these obedient men of God.

CHAPTER 2

Case Study One: Adam

What God said to Adam is the first proven test of man's ability to obey God and keep His commandments.

After God had finished creating the earth and everything including the birds of the air, the fish of the waters and all kinds of animals. Then He said to Himself (God the father, God the son God the Holy Spirit) let us make man in our own image. Genesis 1: 26-27 confirms.

"So God created man in His own image: In the image of God He created him male and female, He created them. The Scripture says God planted a beautiful garden in Eden. A garden is a piece of ground near a dwelling place usually used for growing vegetables, flowers and fruits. Garden is a beautiful thing you know. The Garden of Eden was

1. The first test of responsibility for humanity.
2. The first test of obedience for man. God does not want His children to live a life of idleness. In the Old Testament He charged all His prophets and everyone who follows Him with some sort of responsibility. Moses and Aron were given the task of delivering the children of Israel from bondage in Egypt. Elijah was instructed to go and declare drought in Israel during the time of king Arab. You and I are not different from those who had served the Lord before. God has some responsibility for you to accomplish before He calls

you home. You are equipped to accomplish such responsibility. Have you identified the responsibility God entrusted into your hand? Accomplishing such responsibility is why you are still alive. When Jesus was about to depart this earth to be with His father He said to His followers "Occupy till I come." Luke 19:13; Matthew 28:18-20 "And Jesus came and spoke to them, saying, "All authority has been given to Me in heaven and on earth. Go therefore and make disciples of all the nations, baptizing them in the name of the Father and of the Son and of the Holy Spirit, teaching them to observe all things that I have commanded you; and lo, I am with you always, even to the end of the age." Amen."

Mark 16:15 says "Go into all the world and preach the gospel to every creature." Acts of the Apostles 1: 8c ...You shall be my witnesses in Jerusalem, in all Judaea and Samaria and to the end of the earth."

Jesus clearly charged His disciples to go and win the lost. In the book of 2 Timothy 4:2 says, "Preach the word! Be ready in season and out of season." 2 Thessalonians 3:10 says, "For even when we were with you, we commanded you this: If anyone will not work, neither shall he eat."

God hates laziness. He planted this garden and placed Adam and his wife to be in charge and to tend it. Adam represents the human race. Whatever decisions they made affect us today because we have their blood line, they are our grandparents. The first recorded instruction in the history of man was the instruction God gave to Adam and His wife, "You can eat any fruit inside the garden but "But you must not eat from the tree of knowledge of good and evil for when you eat from it you shall surely die."

The Garden of Eden of our generation is God's inheritance which is people who need to be saved for eternity. God demanded from all of us to make disciples of all nations baptizing them in His name. Sharing the gospel of our Lord Jesus Christ is the highest form of responsibility entrusted to man to accomplish.

Everyone who has personal relationship with Jesus Christ is responsible to share the gospel. Bishops, pastors, teachers of the gospel, elder's, overseas,

Dr., lawyers, prophets, professors etc. I mean every rank and file, no matter your position, you are mandated to participate in this mandate.....love God, love people, and make disciples. Those who lived before us did what God said word for word.

Disobedience to God's commandments or what God said to you is a sin and the results of such sin are physical and spiritual death. You are evidently separated from Him. Separation from His presence is the worst condition anyone can be in. Some general characteristics of obedience to God's word: Obedience to God's commandment shows how much you love God.

- It is a respect to God.
- It is a sign of Submission.
- It is a sign of telling the Lord that you are available for duty.
- It is a sign of willingness to be with the Lord.
- It brings blessing.
- God will trust you
- God will give you eternal life.
- God will reveal to you His secrets. (The secrete things of the Lord is revealed to His children.)
- God will fight for you.
- He will go with you as you go and as come.
- You will be a friend of God.
- Your prayers will be answered promptly.
- You will bear good fruits.
- You will always stay in tune with Him.

Adam heard and understood what God said to Him and was carrying out the responsibility by taking care of the garden. Adam was diligently on duty until Satan showed up through his wife.

Whenever you bent to do exactly what God assigned to you, Satan always shows up in your duty to stop the work of God. He comes in various ways; he may come through friends, family, coworkers, etc. The Bible tells us that Satan has been defeated by our Lord and savior through His death on the Cross. The victory that Jesus won over Satan is our victory today. Jesus Christ gave every believer power and authority over Satan and his agents, and power over all His characteristics. Luke 9: 1 said, "Then He called His twelve disciples together and gave them power and authority over all demons, and to cure diseases."

Satan hates us when we try to do what God said. We can be a successful Christian if we know Jesus Christ in a personal way and do what He said in His word. He hates us even more when he realizes that we know the truth in the word of God. We are to search the Scriptures daily to know what God said in every issue of our life. Paul encourages us to search the scriptures daily. We should go back to the Bible to learn more and more of what God said to us and subsequently walk on it. The word of God should be our lead to everything we are engage to do.

The Scripture said, "Be diligent to present yourself approved to God, a worker who does not need to be ashamed, rightly dividing the word of truth." 2 Timothy 2:15

For Adam, he is the beginning of humanity with responsibilities to take care of, that responsibility is to obey God and care for the garden. When God brought Eve to Adam, He did not go on to rehearse the responsibility but He expected Adam to tutor and encourage his wife on what God said to do it.

I believe Adam clearly gave Eve some tutorials of who God is, and also narrated to her the instructions God gave in relation to taking care of the garden. He probably must have mentioned to Eve the consequences of disobeying God's instructions. "If you eat that fruit, you shall surely die." Unfortunately, Eve fell to the tricks of the devil, this fall was not just for her and her husband but for the generation then and future generations to come.

Beloved disobedience to What God said is sin-- spiritual and physical death. When God said a thing to us, it is our responsibility to strive and do what He said. Doing what He commanded us to do is where the joy of the Lord is.

The Scripture said, "Then the Lord God took [a]the man and put him in the garden of Eden to [b]tend and keep it." Genesis 2:15. God created man first then his wife to help her husband.

Adam as the spiritual leader of his home

God made you the Spiritual leader in your home and will hold you accountable if your family fails to follow God's ways. God made you the leader because He trusts you to lead your family to Him.

You are answerable to God for any misdemeanor in the family. You are to make sure that your family is living for God.

When sin crept into Adam's family, as a result of Eve's crave for new trials for other things. The sin wasn't averted until Jesus came for our rescue. The scripture says, "For all have sinned and fall short of the glory of God." Romans 3:23. When their sin becomes evident, God did not go to Eve but Adam, even though she was the one deceived by Satan. God held Adam responsible for it, and said, "Adam, where are you" God hates sin; however, He loves sinners. This is the ultimate reason for going to the cross to die for us.

As already mentioned, the whole idea of why God created Eve was to have Eve help Adam and to encourage him as he carries out his assignment. "Help" a key word in Eve assignment. She was not made to compete with the man. She is not to be the active one but to stand solidly with her husband. Another reason for bringing Eve to Adam was to help him and encourage him for fellowships. The relationship is not for competition. It was not to be without fellowship with the Lord. God gave you the spiritual responsibility to encourage and bring your wife and children to Him. The scripture said that God looked and said it is not good for man to be alone; I will make him a helper. Man was created to provide for his family. God spoke to the man after he was created and put him in the garden to care for it. Wives are made to be a helper. A helper is someone who willingly assists in doing something. God holds every man responsible for:

1. Achieving God's plan for himself
2. Achieve God's purpose.
3. Prevent fall of humanity.

God did not just speak in general to humanity but spoke specifics things to man. I remember a few years ago that I was about to walk into some hundreds of angry demonstrators and mob residence of a city. They were so angry that they were destroying things; this was as a result of government's increase in the price of petroleum. As I was driving in the opposite direction towards them, I heard the inner witness of the Holy Spirit and said, "Do you love me" my answer was yes, I do, and then, He said "praise me". Instinctively I did and continued until I saw a mob of about five hundred to one thousand people coming towards my direction. I heard the whispering of the Holy Spirit saying turn right into a mini-mall on the right, and I did as He said. The surging mob passed by the major road, then I pulled out into the major road and continued on my way. It was then I felt in my Spirit that it was God's urgent rescue. It is absolutely important to pay attention and be alert in your Spirit to recognize the voice of the Holy Spirit.

God speaks to you at all times, while you are in the bank, shopping, at a gas station, or driving, while you are sitting or standing, even while in the shower or getting dressed. I got the title of some the books I wrote while I was driving. There is no set place purposed for God to say something to you. God is actively working for you. He is involved in the plan of your life. He never leaves you nor forsakes you. Successful relation with God starts by:

1. Faith in His only begotten son Jesus Christ. Jesus is the way to the Father. Jesus Himself said, "I am the way, the truth, and the life. No one comes to the Father except through Me" John 14:6.
2. Then study the scripture and constantly apply what you learn to your daily lifestyle. When God speaks, He expects you and me to listen and obey. The scripture says, "If you love Me, [a]keep My commandments. 16 And I will pray the Father, and He will give you another Helper, that He may abide with you forever" John

14:15-16. Obedience is compliance with an order, request, or law or submission to another's authority. (Online Bible dictionary)

We must practice to walk in the Spirit. Walking in the Spirit means relying by faith on the guidance of the Holy Spirit in thought, word, and in actions. You do not make decision without the counsel meeting with Him.

- Rely on Him before you pick up the phone to answer a call.
- Rely on Him before you take any exams.
- Rely on Him before you choose a particular profession.
- Rely on Him before you embark on any project.
- Rely on Him before you embark on a marriage relationship.

Always wait for an answer before you proceed to take action. His answers sometimes are not instant. One of the good qualities of true believers of Jesus Christ is patience. He will tell you what to do and how to do it. God loves His children, who walk closely with Him. He honors those who recognizes Him as their source of all things.

God spoke to Adam, Noah. Abraham, Isaac, Jacob, Elijah, the Prophets, the Seers, and all whom He chose to fulfill His purpose. They are the leaders, they spoke and prophesied the mind of God to the people, and what they spoke is established, and the name of God is glorified. What God said to them was passed on from generation to generation. They heard God's voice; they believed Him and acted on what He said, then result was achieved as the people for whom the word meant for were blessed. If you act on what God said to you, you will be blessed, and the community will be blessed as well.

Prophet Elijah declared a drought, "As the Lord God of Israel lives, before whom I stand, there shall not be dew nor rain these years, except at my word." 1 Kings 17:1. Verse continued, Then the Lord said to Elijah, "Get away from here and turn eastward, and hide by the Brook Cherith, which flows into the Jordan. 4 And it will be that you shall drink from the brook, and I have commanded the ravens to feed you there."

Verse 5 says Elijah obeyed the voice of the Lord. The above passage is one of the examples of how to be a true servant of God here on earth. Obedience is the main key to pleasing God. His indwelling presence helps us to fulfill our assignments. Yes, He participates in every step of doing what He tells us to do.

Whenever God sends you on assignment, He equips you with things needed to bring good results effectively. If the church can recognize the indwelling of the Holy Spirit in their life, I strongly believe that the church will be more effective in populating the kingdom of God. We will have more saints getting involved in Evangelism, and more in missionary work to the nations of the world, including countries that are hostile to the Christian faith.

God provided everything to His followers needed to effectively carry out their assignments. Those who do what God said are leaders in every sphere of life. They are the foundation for good governance. They initiate good programs for the government and direct its affairs as well. The ruling governments rely on their instructions for their day to day governance. They were able to achieve all this because of their reliance on God and obedience to what God said. They are men of God through which God speaks the nations. The God of Old Testament is the same as New Testament sections of the Bible; He is worthy of all prayers and worships—His name is Jesus Christ. Can God trust you today?

We are always quick to point out someone's mistakes and place a judgement on him for failures. No one is without mistakes, no one is without sins. The Scripture said, "For all have sinned and fall short of the glory of God" Romans 3:23. The Bible also said, "Judge not, that you be not judged. For with what judgment you judge, you will be judged; and with the measure you use, it will be measured back to you. And why do you look at the speck in your brother's eye, but do not consider the plank in your own eye?" Matthew 7:1-3.

The sin of Adam ran through our blood line, because we are his offspring-- they are our grandparents. The only thing that can take our sins away and cleanse us forever is the Blood of Jesus Christ.

"But if we walk in the light as He is in the light, we have fellowship with one another, and the blood of Jesus Christ His Son cleanses us from all sin." 1 John 1:7.

Whenever we disobey God's commandments, we ardently align ourselves to the same disobedience as that of Adam and Eve. Each time we sin, we invariably disrespects God. He sees our behavior as being rebellious and lacking of love for God. Adam failed to follow through to what God said to him. Adam disobeyed God when:

1. He ate the particular fruit God said do not eat. Genesis 3:6
2. Adam listened and followed his wife's suggestions instead of God's instructions.
3. He was not sensitive to the Spirit of God.
4. He gave excuses instead of owning the responsibility of what he did. (The woman you gave to be with me, she gave me and I ate it. Genesis 3.) In addition, Adam failed to confess or ask for forgiveness.

The sin of Adam and Eve has been the cause of human calamity from generation to generation to this day. The primary reason Jesus came to the work was to save us from the sin of Adam. As we already mentioned, we all inherited the consequences of their actions. We are all sinners right from birth, in sin, are we conceived.

Sometime ago, I happened to run into a gentleman who I had wanted to introduce Jesus Christ to. Before I could get into the details of sharing the good news, he excused me to ask a question. He said where God was when people were suffering, where was God when someone picked up a gun and shot people who were enjoying their evening concert, he went on and on until he was exhausted.

Then I said to him that the answer to his question is simple: we have all refused to allow God to be a part of our lives. Tell me if you refused God's offer of love and to care for you, is it not Satan you made yourselves available to? Yes, if you recognize Him as God, if you call upon Him in a time of trouble, He will answer you. He will show you a way out of whatever is troubling you. Come near to Him, and He will come near to you. When you refuse God in your life, then Satan comes in and takes over. Unless you repent, you likewise perish.

Therefore, Satan has a field day using his agents to fulfill his agenda. Jesus said that He has come that we might have life and that we might have it more abundantly. But Satan comes to kill, steal, and destroy. John 10:10.

As we were getting deeper into our conversation, his bus pulled up. As the conversation progressed, he sat unspeaking for a while. I do believe that the Holy Spirit was bringing conviction to his heart before to his bus pulled up.

You see, consequences of Eve's romance with Satan brought the down fall of her husband, who also participated in eating the forbidden fruit. The overall result is what we are experiencing in our world that is "SIN." In our generation, every negativity we see today like death, lack, sickness, poverty, failure, wars, lies, etc. are the result of sins. Jesus said "He had overcome the world." John 16:33. Yes, He had overcome all these negativities battling our lives.

The Bible made us to understand that the Lord came to Adam in the cool of the evening to fellowship and to instruct them. God had said a lot of things to Adam, but He specifically said to Adam.

"BUT OF THE TREE OF THE KNOWLEDGE OF GOOD AND EVIL YOU SHALL NOT EAT, FOR IN THE DAY THAT YOU EAT OF IT YOU SHALL SURELY DIE." Genesis 2:17.

The above statement in Genesis 2:17 was what God said to Adam specifically.

Factors which made Adam disobey God.

God carefully informed Adam of the consequences of disobedience, and that death is the imminent result of not doing what God said. So the question is why did Adam went ahead and disobeyed God even though he knew the consequences. Whatever made Adam to do what He did is the same factor that drives us to sin against God today. There are five factors we can look at:

a. Seeing. You see first, then
b. You Desire
c. Deceit. Satan brings in deception in your mind.
d. Decision. Satan's lies bring conviction in your mind
e. Action. You then go-ahead to do the particular suggestion he gave to you.

These five factors are the powerful elements, which Satan uses to lure people to sin against God. Satan went to Eve and deceived Eve. Eve's conviction to eat the forbidden fruit was the same channel through which her husband failed. Eve went to her husband, who agreed with his wife's suggestions to eat the fruit. Everything that Satan does with us is through our minds. One of the Satan's characteristics is lies. His words of suggestions sound like truth, but are lies. The only proven solution to escaping his suggestions is our dependence on God and His words. If you are a person who depends God's word in your daily orientation, then God will keep you safe from falling into Satan's traps. You should also be able to know when he comes with his tricks to deceive. You see, first, he came to Eve as she was looking at the fruits. Secondly, he let Eve desire in her heart to have it. Then, he deceived her into eating the fruit and that she shall not surely die. Eve made an immediate decision to eat the fruit. She physically plucked the Fruit and ate and gave some to her husband as well.

When Satan sees that action has taken place, he stands by the side knowing that his mission has been completed. He will now stand to laugh at you as you go through the consequences of your decision. We are to renew our mind daily and meditate on it. If we sincerely do this, then we are fully prepared to counteract his suggestions to disobey God.

As already stated, Satan is the real antagonist of Jesus Christ, who robs others of God's blessings to procure himself dominion over humankind and corporeality. We must remember the expiatory sacrifice of Jesus Christ and do what God to you—be obedient to God's word.

So my question beloved of God is what did God said to you since you became aware of His existence. Your reaction to whatever He said to you is what determines who you are to Him. Adam heard God clearly; he was obedient to Him in the onset until his wife showed up. I see it that maybe Adam did not properly lecture and impart into Eve the seriousness or the consequences of failure to carryout God's commandment word to word. Eve's failure to adhere to the theological of the season brought the down fall of her husband and consequent fall of humanity and separation from God.

God had made us aware of what sin is. He then commanded us to flee from sin and its likeness.

In Matthew 5:22 says, "For it is more profitable for you that one of your members perish, than for your whole body to be cast into hell." The scripture informs us that God loves us but hates the sin in us, so to further deliver us, He gave to us (the World) His only begotten son Jesus Christ so that whosoever believe in Him shall not perish but have everlasting life. John 3:16.

The problem of sin is still here, but there is also a solution in the person Jesus Christ. If you believe Jesus Christ and invite Him into your life to be your personal Lord and savior, the scripture says "You will be saved." Romans 10:9.

The consequences of sin are always disastrous. The scripture says that the wage of sin is death, but the gift of God is eternal life in Christ Jesus Christ. Romans 6:23.

God does not condone sin. Your sin and mine was the reason Jesus Christ was nailed to the Cross! Sin separates us from God. God speaking through Prophet Isaiah in Isaiah, 59:1-2b, saying:

"Behold, the Lord's hand is not shortened, That it cannot save; Nor His ear heavy, That it cannot hear. But your iniquities have separated you from your God, And your sins have hidden His face from you, So that He will not hear." The connection between God and us was broken as a result of sin of Adam, which started from the Garden of Eden. So beloved Jesus Christ came to bridge the gap we had with God. You are brought near to God if you believe and confess the sacrifice Jesus did on the cross. Inviting Jesus in your life as Lord and savior gives as access to Trinity.

Did God say something to you?

A lot of people when posed with this question, gets confused. Some said yes, God spoke to them while others said not yet, others said "I don't know". What will be your answer if you are posed with the same question? As a believer of Jesus Christ, my answer is "yes". It is important to remember that God has spoken to everyone who has confessed Jesus Christ as Lord and savior. It will be a denial of your faith in the Lord to deny the fact that God hasn't spoken to you. As already mentioned above, God started speaking to man since the creation of Man. As already discussed, God spoke to things He created, then Adam in the Garden of Eden. He said to them what He wants them to do. The instructions that God gave to Adam stand as the first test of obedience to our God; instead, they did opposite of what God said to them to do, thereby falling into the deception of the devil, which resulted to total damnation of humanity.

The result of the disobedience is what we are suffering from today. But God, through His Love sent Jesus Christ to die for our sins. Ephesians 2:8 says "For by grace you have been saved through faith, and that not of yourselves; it is the gift of God."

CHAPTER 3

Case study Two: Noah

What God said to Noah?

As the population of the world continues to multiply, sin of Adam began to showcase in the lives of the People; everyone wants to do what pleases him. There was wickedness of diverse concern which are boldly portrayed in the behavior of the people. There's no visible evidence of the fear of God. The punishment God meted out to Adam and Eve was sending them out of the garden as a result of their disobedience.

It did not affect/change in their behavior towards God. As mentioned, the sins of man separate the mind from God. Disobedience is like a taboo in the eyes of God. So God said within Himself, "Then the Lord saw that the wickedness of man was great in the earth, and that every intent of the thoughts of his heart was only evil continually. And the Lord was sorry that He had made man on the earth, and He was grieved in His heart. So the Lord said, "I will destroy man whom I have created from the face of the earth, both man and beast, creeping thing and birds of the air, for I am sorry that I have made them." But Noah found grace in the eyes of the Lord." Genesis.6: 5-8.

The above passage reveals to us how much God reviews the earth and everything He has made. He supervises everything to make sure things are working according to the order in which He originally placed them.

The Scripture said that His Spirit lives in us, to help us live a godly life. He reveals to us day to day how to be obedient to the glory of His name. The Psalmist tells us that the earth is the Lord's and everything in it. Psalm 24. My question is, have you found favor in the eyes of the Lord? Favor is an act of kindness. Have you seen God's favor on you? Yes, when God chooses you, He trusts you, and when He trusts you, He reveals His mind to you. God reveals what He wants to do, then what He wants you to do. When God tells you His mind then He will tell you what to do.

"The end of all flesh has come before me, for the earth is filled with violence through them; and behold, I will destroy them with the earth. Make yourself an ark of gopher wood; make rooms in the ark and cover the inside and outside with pitch....." Genesis 6: 13-14. Noah strictly obeyed what God said to him.

If you obey what God said to you, in the Bible, your life will spiritually be transformed into a better and more productive Christ-like lifestyle. He will trust you for bigger things to the glory of His name. God's Presence will encompass you and your family.

The result of Noah's obedience.

The Bible categorically declared that Noah was a preacher of righteousness, 2 Peter 2:5. We were told that Noah evangelized his family. In other words, Noah told his family the things that are of utmost importance to God, and that is to love Him and keep His commandments. Putting your faith in Jesus Christ and allowing him in your life as your Lord and savior is an imperative factor for practicing and expressing God's obedience. Noah loved God, and it was accounted to him for righteousness. Noah did as God instructed him and he and his family were saved form the flood, which destroyed the whole world. As a result of Noah's obedience, God spared him and his family; this is how God bestows his blessings on someone who listens to him and obeys him in every walk of life. The Bible said that God knows how to keep His people safe in the midst of the sinful world. God, who kept Noah, will also keep you to make sure you make it to the end. Yes, He sees you through if you obey His words.

Question.

My 15 years old daughter Gift, was by my side while I was writing about Noah. I asked her, "What did she think Noah did wrong while serving the Lord?" She answered, "Noah should have brought more people to the Ark, instead of his family alone."

The answer she gave to the question spoke to my heart directly. Humankind is bound to perish and if you are true believer of Jesus Christ it is your responsibility to invite people to Him. So, how many people have you led to invite Jesus Christ to be their personal Lord and savior?

How many people have you explained the plan of salvation according to the Scripture with the intention of helping them to experience eternal life just like you did? We are saved to save. If you are not winning the lost or encouraging the ministry of Evangelism then your total Christian experience should be rebooted. You need to make soul winning the soul your first priority.

Sometimes we may be tempted to gravitate towards the dictation of the flesh, to approach our work with the Lord in a certain way contrary to the biblical standard. Noah did not hesitate but swung into action to inform them of God's intentions to destroy the earth as a result of sins. Noah obeyed God's word, and even ministered to his family as well, resulting in that his family was saved while the other people who did not confess and believe the Lord were destroyed in the flood. His obedience led to salvation of his family, who became the faithful generation which we are part of. In contrast, Noah's Ark is a vessel of salvation. The ark portrays the theophany of Jesus Christ in the Old Testament. You and your family will be blessed if you obey What God said to you.

Noah's Ark, a type of Jesus Christ.

There are six distinct ways Noah's Ark is seen as a Type of Jesus Christ.

1. God commanded Noah and his family to go into the ark, or it will be too late. As they all ran into the Ark, they were all saved as the flood of destruction descended. All other creatures were destroyed, those who ran into the Ark was saved. Genesis 6:13-14.

In the New Testament, Jesus saves those who came to God through Him. Romans 10:9 says, "If you confess with your mouth the Lord Jesus and believe in your heart that God has raised Him from the dead, you will be saved." All that was said to Noah; he obeyed. As a result, Noah and his family were saved.

Those who believe the Lord were saved, but those who refused were destroyed with the flood. The grace of God is still available for today if you run to Jesus.

2. Ark of the New Testament (Jesus Christ) is the only way to be saved.

Jesus is the only escape route for sinners. "There is no other name given among men under heaven by which we may be saved, but the name of Jesus Christ." God provided these escape routes because:

a. He loves us. John 3:16, "For God so loved the world that He gave His only begotten Son, so that whosoever believes in Him should not perish but have everlasting life."

b. You are in His image. Genesis 1:26

c. He wants those who will follow His footsteps.

God revealed to Noah what he was about to do. "The end of all flesh has come before Me, for the earth is filled with violence through them; and behold, I will destroy them with the earth." Genesis 6:13.

God then gave Noah the specific instructions on what to do. Noah did not argue but obeyed every word that God spoke to him. Noah did not follow his personal consciousness or experience, but God's step by step orders. I will like to emphasize that whenever you are doing for the Lord, it is important to know that God will not leave you to complete the task alone, He is with you all the way through until the particular assignment is fully completed.

God said to Joshua, Moses's assistance, "....... As I have been with Moses so shall I be with you, Joshua" 1:5b. God never leaves us alone, and He constantly watches over you. His love and mercy always encompass us.

d. God wants to preserve those who will take care of His inheritance. God's inheritance is His people. He invested a lot in you. Jesus shed His precious blood so that you and I can live a life free of sins. He prepared for us in advance eternal life in Him. He has our mansion ready, waiting for us to accomplish our assignments and to come and occupy our mansion with Him. You are destined to spend eternity with Him unless you refuse. The choice is yours.

e. He wants those who will reach out with the gospel to the perishing world, and make disciples of all nations, not church attendants or bench warmers in the church. Are you leading people to Christ? In one way or the other, you must be adding souls to the kingdom of God. Hear the word of; Ezekiel 3:18-19, "When I say to the wicked, you shall surely die, and you give him no warning nor speak to warn the wicked from his wicked way to save his life, that wicked man shall die in his iniquity;, but his blood will I require from your hand yet, if you warn the wicked, and he does not turn from his wickedness nor from his wicked way, he shall die in his iniquity, but you have delivered your soul."

God designed the Ark; man did not design it.

Man did not plan for our deliverance-- God did. God planned man's way of escape before the foundation of the world by sending to the world our only means of salvation from the sins of the world.

Your salvation has already been put in place before you were born. (Jeremiah 1:1). Our responsibility is to believe and trust in Him.

3. Ark saved Noah and his family from God's flood. They were all confidently inside the Ark enjoying their day to day activities as the rest of the world of sin was destroyed by the flood.

Jesus was sent to save the world from sin. He is our shelter in the time of storm. If you confess with your mouth the Lord Jesus Christ and believe in your heart that God raised Him from the dead, you will be saved. Romans 10:9. Jesus Christ is our savior. The Ark had only one door through which everyone was supposed to go inside; Jesus Christ is the only door to eternal life. Jesus Himself said,

"I am the door: by me if any man enter in, he shall be saved, and shall go in and out, and find pasture."

4. Just as God revealed His intentions to Noah and asked Noah to come into the Ark, He also revealed His intentions to save the world from sin. He mandated us to do the same as well. Jesus spoke through Mark, "Go into all the world and preach the gospel to every creature." Mark 16:15.

Once the door of the ark was closed, there was no one to come in. Beloved, this is the day of salvation; the second coming of Jesus Christ is much closer than we can imagine. We are to hold unto Him, watch and pray, and do what He said.

Isaiah's warning states, "Seek the Lord while He May be found, call Upon Him while He is near." Isaiah 55:6.

5. Just as the coming of the flood and destruction of the world were revealed to Noah so was the second coming of Jesus Christ was revealed to the saints (Those who have Faith in Jesus). The date and time of the flood were not known just as the date and time of the second coming of Jesus are unknown. The Bible made us understand that He will come like a thief in the night at unexpected time and unpredictable season. Some will be marrying and giving in marriage. Some will be partying, others in the field

farming and suddenly the trumpet sounds signifying the arrival of our savior Jesus Christ.

Beloved what will you be doing, or what do you think of doing when the trumpet sounds.

6. When Noah and his family entered the ark God closed the door, those who refused to enter, those who were hesitating to enter, those who said they are not ready, and those who said not today were left behind to face the destructive force of God's flood.

I pray that will not be in the category of people who were left behind, and that you will be ready in the name of Jesus Christ.

People have various reasons why they refuse or postpone to receive Jesus Christ as Lord and savior. Some of those reasons are penned above as we encounter them each time we present the gospel to someone in the street or door to door Evangelism. If you are a witness, I believe that you must have experienced the same excuses not to invite Jesus in their life as Lord and savior.

CHAPTER 4

Case Study Three: Abraham

The Book of Genesis covers most of the story on Abraham. Perhaps he was one of the most reverend people in the Bible. He was known because of his faith in God. God spoke to him, Abraham heard and acted on what God said. Abraham was a man just like you and me, and He had a father and a mother just like us. He lived and grew like we did. So what is so special about him? Why do we call him the father of faith? Why did God call him His friend? Why do we sing a song that is attributed to his success in service to the almighty God? I believe the best way to answer this question is to look at his relationship with God, and the way when God spoke to him. With such information, we will be able to live a life that pleases the Lord, just like Abraham did. He was living with his family in the town called Ur of Chaldeans when he heard God's voice saying,

"Get out of your country, From your family And from your father's house, To a land that I will show you. I will make you a great nation; I will bless you And make your name great; And you shall be a blessing. I will bless those who bless you, And I will curse him who curses you; And in you all the families of the earth shall be blessed." Genesis 12:1-3.

Before the word of God come to Abraham:

1. He was not popular/famous.
2. He lived among pagans with his family.

3.   Abraham was not rich.
4.   Abraham's name was not great.
5.   He was not blessings to anybody.
6.   He was 75 years old when he left his country.
7.   His name was Abram.

His covenant name became Abraham because he did what God said to him.

God trusted him and gave him a new name to what we know as Abraham. We should note this seriously that before God called Abraham out for service, Abraham and his family worshiped Idols. (Joshua 24:2.) We are not informed how knowledgeable Abraham was about one true God, but we do know that Abraham was religious in some ways.

His father, Terah, was a worshiper of idols. They may be involved in other human religious matters such as the philosophy of life and other human affairs. Also in the other school of thoughts, Terah's Catechism may have told him about the true God and how he delivered the children of Israel from Egypt. He heard about the destruction of the world with the flood, he may have also learnt how God in Heaven saved his grandfather, Noah and his family. He may have heard this story from his father Terah. He may have told him how God hated sins, which God called "wicked heart" to those who indulged in it. Jeremiah 17:9.

Abraham may have learnt that worship of Idols and other forms of sins was the reason God destroyed the world with a flood. Abraham was comfortable to whatsoever he was doing before God called him. The ultimate point remains that Abraham heard what God, and he responded and obeyed. He followed word for word God's instructions as Abraham was determined to obey God no matter what.

The world we live in, the life we lead, is shifting towards godlessness and antagonism for God. We have all done our own things, worship who we want to worship, and do what pleases us. We are completely aback from the almighty God.

My point is when we heard what God said, what did we do with it? Our reaction to what God said determines how much we love Him. Like Abraham, God will change our status, and give us a new name and new life if we trust and obey Him. First, obedience to God is to trust Him through His son Jesus Christ.

The Scripture declared, "He who has the Son has life; he who does not have the Son of God does not have life." 1 John 5:12. Jesus said, "I am the resurrection and the life. He who believes in Me, though he may die, he shall live" John 11:25. Abraham heard clearly what God said to him. He did not consider his comfortable environment, his friends, his relatives, his culture, his favorite hangouts, but decided to do what God said. He was not in any way intimate with God's principles before he heard the voice of God. He was consumed in his immediate culture of worship of his family Idol. Abraham willed within himself to obey. His heart was willing to obey God despite all odds surrounding him led to:

1. God approved of Abraham's genuine love for Him.

Abraham's obedience to what God said to him showed how much he loved God. Jesus declared in one of His sermons, "If you love Me, keep My commandments. And I will pray the Father, and He will give you another Helper, that He may abide with you forever— the Spirit of truth, whom the world cannot receive, because it neither sees Him nor knows Him; but you know Him, for He dwells with you and will be in you." John 14:15-17 Comforter in the text is His Holy Spirit, every genuine obedience to God's calling brings God's special blessings of His Holy Spirit to abide in you. He is there to help you accomplish His plan for your life. His comforter, who is also known as "Advocate," will advocate for you in every area of your life. You are God's special man or woman; yes, God's presence will indwell you continually throughout your life to keep you from falling. He will also remind you of everything about God so you can live for Him alone. Have you experienced the presence of the Holy Spirit in your life? If you do, one of the clear signs is your love for God and your willingness to obey God despite the affliction you are going through. If you do not experience His presence, you can invite Him today. Surely, He will come and indwell you and give you the joy of salvation. Jesus was specific when He said if you love me, keep my commandment. Can you categorically say you love God? If your answer is yes it then means that:

- You have received Jesus Christ into your life by faith. You keep His commandments.
- You practice living righteously according to His words. You love your neighbor and point Jesus Christ to them. You willingly engaged in Evangelism.
- Forgive those who have offended you.

It is very easy for you and me to say we love God, but in actual fact, we don't.

1. God trusted him and called him His friend.

The popular saying in the Bible still goes on today, "Abraham, the friend of God," and there is a song that goes with it. I am a friend of God because he calls me His friend. And the scripture was fulfilled that says, "Abraham believed God, and it was accounted to him for righteousness." And he was called the friend of God." James 2:23. God called Abraham, a Friend because of his obedience. Since Abraham knew obedience was the ultimate way to get closer to God, his love for God became the reason he was called the friend of God. God will also call you His friend if you do what He said. You can show your love for God if you invite His only begotten Son Jesus Christ into your life by faith as your personal Lord and savior (Romans 10:9, John 1:12.) then live in obedience to what He said to you daily in His words.

2. God revealed His awesome personality to Him.

As Abraham followed and obeyed God's commandments step by step, God then revealed His awesome characteristics to him. Abraham's qualities in faith, obedience, hospitality, and intercession make him eligible as a friend of God. He was blessed beyond measure in everything. Genesis 14:18-19; Genesis21:22. He worshipped God. Genesis 21:33. He had faith in God.

Genesis 15:6; Romans 4: 18-22, Hebrew 6:15. He was a prophet and intercessor; Genesis 20-7.

3. Abraham became very rich and famous in the land. Genesis 21:22. Genesis 24:35;

Abraham was rich in cattle and in men and women servants.

4. Abraham become very powerful militarily.

He became so powerful that other nations and individuals were scared of him. Through the power of God, He conquered the Canaanites and maintained independence from them.

5. Abraham enquired of God in all that he wanted to do or accomplish. He agreed with God in all things and followed through in all that God wanted him to do.

Abraham's unadulterated love and faith in God drew God's attention and trust on him. You can be that one today. God wants unadulterated belief and faith in His promises, then He can trust you for greater things and will call you His friend. He is no respecter of persons and everyone is equal in the eyes of God. If He can trust Abraham, He can also trust you and me, and will fulfill all His promises for us if we obey and do what he said to us.

Practical lessons from the Abraham Believe:

Belief is one of the most important approaches in the life of every Christian and non-Christians. Belief is just to accept something as true, or to feel sure of the truth. From the time that God called Abraham out of his family to a different geographical location, Abraham heard what God said, he believed and followed through to obey Him in all things.

If you and I want an unadulterated relationship with God then we must believe Him in His word; the Bible detailed us about God. God is not an imaginary being, and if we search for Him in His word, we will find Him. If you faithfully call on Him, He will answer you and meet your needs. It is the responsibility of every Christian to believe and search for Him in the Bible. We can only come to know Him by studying the Bible. If you are one those who don't read up on Bible and its chronicles, you might end up with a myopic view about God. The book of the Hebrews declares, "But without faith it is impossible to please Him, for he who comes to God must believe that He is, and that He is a rewarder of those who diligently seek Him." Hebrews 11:6b.

What was Abraham's Foundation of faith that made him to believe God immediately after he heard what God said? To answer this question, I think we are to refer back to his grandfather, Noah. Noah was a faithful man of God. The Bible declares of him; Noah found favor in the eyes of the Lord, and it was accounted for him as righteous. Noah and his family were the only ones saved when they entered the Ark as it rained for 40 days and 40 nights, and the entire earth was covered with water. The story of the Ark must be one of the motivating factors that revealed the true God to Abraham. As already said, it helps to build up a belief in the life of Abraham. Again we can learn from story of the Ark thus:

- Grace of God in action to deliver humanity from eternal destruction.
- The only true way to escape the punishment of sin is the Ark (A type of Jesus).
- Ark was the only hope of escape from sins. (Jesus Christ is the only hope of escape from sin). "If you confess with your mouth the Lord Jesus and believe in your heart that God has raised Him from the dead, you will be saved." Roman 10:9.

Abraham also believed the story of how God delivered the people of Israel from their bondage in Egypt. We all believed in God and praised Him as we read this demonstration of God's power. Abraham heard the same story because the incident happened prior to His generation. Also, he may have read or was told about God's deliverance of his people from bondage. God's act in creation and saving of humanity is a defining factor that demonstrated His Omnipotence and strengthened Abraham's belief in God. Abraham saw God's goodness and love to all creation, so he trusted Him and was blessed.

Not only did Abraham believed in God, but he also had Faith. We must learn to believe Him in His word and do all that He said to us.

Faith.

As already stated, the stories about God's love to His people principled Abraham to believe in God unequivocally. Abraham believed in the existence of true God. He applied faith in God's promises, and God rewarded him generously for his righteousness. Faith is complete trust in someone or something. Abraham's Faith skyrocketed as a result of God's practical demonstration of His faithfulness and power. Abraham received God's promises over and over as a result of his application God's Rhema words. Secondly, he read about God's creation, such as Adam and Eve, and God's mercy to save man from sins. All these put together gave Abraham insights of whom God is. He constantly sought God, and obeyed what God said to him.

We are to be sensitive to the things of God and obey all that He said to us. Obedience is the only way to please Him. Through "Obedience," we can have full knowledge of the Trinity (God the father, the Son and Holy Spirit.). We must allow the word of God to rule our lives.

We must follow the footsteps of Jesus Christ as much as we can, and practice living as per those word. Study the Bible daily.

Let the word of God be your compass at all times, both in your decisions and your walk with Him. The scripture declares, "Let the word of God dwell in you richly." Applying God's word in every walk of life completes the faith of believer and fulfills the purpose for which God sent us. He is all-knowing; He knows whether we are there just to make up the number of worshipers or pray for true salvation. His Spirit will lead us in every circumstance as He promised that He never leaves us nor forsakes us,.

Hebrews 13:5.The evidence of the presence of the Holy Spirit is seen in you when you truly walk with Him. Are you been led by the Holy Spirit of God?

Remember, Abraham was empowered and led by the Holy Spirit as a result of his obedience to God's commandments. Do you need the power and the presence of God in your life? Then obey His commands. Proverbs 3:5; 6, 7, 8 encourages us, "Trust in the Lord with all your heart, And lean not on your own understanding; In all your ways acknowledge Him, And He shall direct your paths." Do not be wise in your own eyes fear the Lord and shun evil, and this will bring health to your body and nourishment to your bones.

CHAPTER 5

Case Study Four: Moses

As we continue with our discussion on "what God said," it might be the right time to bring Moses's life and chronicles into focus as our case study. We will want to know what Moses did when he heard what God said to him, which made him a great man of God in the Bible.

Moses was one of the reputable characters discussed in the Bible, precisely in the book of Exodus. A saying goes that "Reputation is what people know about you, but Character is what God knows about you." Moses was a prominent prophet, who, because of his unusual beginning as a prophet of God, was inclusive in the theological education as a prophet of God. Moses was raised in a king's palace, king Pharaoh of Egypt. Even though Moses was raised in the king's house-hold, he knew without a doubt that he was a Hebrew, an Israelite. He saw the punishment meted out to the Jews, so he took a stand to defend them in every given opportunity. In the process of his action, he murdered an Egyptian who was fighting a fellow Israelite. When this crime was exposed, and following this, He became become afraid for of his life, for he thought the king Pharaoh would kill him. Therefore, he decided to flee to Midian and married Jethro's daughter. He became son In-Law to the Jethro, the priest of Midian. He employed Moses to tend to his flocks. Moses was on this assignment until God met him and said something to him.

Then Moses led the flock and came to Horeb, the mount of God. It was while Moses was on duty attending to the flocks in the field that he noticed an unusual occurrence where he saw a burning bush, but the bush was not burning. Moses was intrigued by the nature of the fire, so he decided to go closer to see this mysterious event. It was when he drew near to the burning bush that God said something to Moses.

God is a master planner. In fact, in Jeremiah 1:5 God said, "Before I formed you in the womb I knew you; Before you were born I sanctified you; I ordained you a prophet to the nations."

God knows you and me before the foundation of the world. He already planned our life the way it should be; that is why God commanded us to depend on Him for His plan of our life is in His hands. There's no two-way about it. God knows how to get our attention. It may not be through a burning bush, but in some ways, God has called you into the Ministry. The earlier you realize the calling of God in your life, the sooner you will began to enjoy the benefits of your obedience to Him.

God got my attention when my wife and I had bitter experience waiting for the fruit of the womb. It was during this period in our lives that God spoke to me through His words, prophecies, and the inner witness of the Holy Spirit.

By nature I was born a shy person; I couldn't even hold a discussion of any type with anyone. My shyness and inability to communicate effectively hundred preaching, but with divine Glory, He delivered me from this introverted behaviour. He revealed His awesome presence over and over again and assured me of His guidance and protection. He did not stop here; rather, He sent me to a couple of people to tell them to repent from religiosity and receive Jesus Christ as Lord and savior. God knew it wouldn't be an easy task for me to carry out, which is why He sent a pastor to accompany me to the homes of those individuals. He made it a little easier for me by commanding that the pastor should not say a word and that I should deliver the message by myself. After this simple act of obedience was done, my life was never the same. This assignment not only counteracted my introverted behaviour, it also brought me closer to the Lord. I begin to love the things of God, and enjoy fellowship with other believers. I attend the church on my own, I and read the Bible at all times. It was amazing how God cleaned me up for His purpose. I don't know about you, but I am pretty sure that God had said something to you. Have you carried it out?

Not only did God make my calling clearer, but He also equipped me with abilities I never thought I could have, which included leading people to Jesus Christ. God made in me a spiritually progressive Christian. Today, I am so thankful to God to lead me all the way even to become the author of six Christian classic books, glory be to His name. It all started when God said something to you, and you follow through with it. Obedience to God's Word brings blessings, both spiritual and physical blessings. As already stated, God tests our love for Him through our obedience to His instructions, "You are My friends if you do whatever I command you." John 15:14.

The Man Moses

1. Do not draw near this place. Take your sandals off your feet, for the place where you stand is the holy ground. I am the God of your father-- the God of Abraham, the God of Isaac, and the God of Jacob." I have surely seen the oppression of my people who are in Egypt, and have heard their cry because of their taskmasters, for I know their sorrows, so I have come down to deliver them out of the hand of the Egyptians, and to bring them up from that land to a good and large land-- a land flowing with milk and honey, to a place of the Canaanites and Hittites and the Amorites and the Perizzites and the Hivites and the Jebusites. Now therefore, behold the cry of children of Israel has come to me, and I have seen the oppression with which the Egyptians oppress them. Come now, therefore, and I will send you to Pharaoh that you may bring my people out of Egypt.

The above passage is a specific word of God to Moses or Rheama's word to Moses. Moses willingly responded to what God said to him. God trusted him and progressed further to discuss Israelites deliverance from Pharaoh, the king of Egypt. When you obey God and do what he says to you, He will trust you and back you up with His presence. He will reveal to you His secrets. Do you know that God has secrets which are uncovered to us? No wonder the Bible stated in Deuteronomy 29:29, "The secret things belong to the Lord our God, but those things which are revealed belong to us and to our children forever, that we may do all the words of this law." Also, the word of God as written in 1 John 4:4 will apply to you, "You are of God, little children, and have overcome them, because He who is in you is greater than he who is in the world." God will answer your enemies for you and keep their evil thoughts and plans far from you and your family. He warns your enemies of the consequences of their actions while keeping you away from spiritual and physical afflictions, "God is our refuge and strength, a very present help in trouble." Psalm 46:1. Do you know that you are anointed of God? You walk around daily with the power and presence of God inside of you. Yes, beloved, God built in you what it takes to be a unique individual. You are chosen for God's purpose, His inheritance, for which He came from heaven. He did what no one can do, and He took the most painful way in order to set you free from eternal damnation in hell fire—all praise to His grace because which you are alive and well at the moment. As already stated, you are in covenant with the Lord through His shed blood (Matthew 26:28). Your faith in the rising savior has equipped you to be anointed and a prophet of God. You are God's agent to proclaim the salvation to humanity. You are chosen through your faith to counteract anything that might stand in the way of salvation of His people. Through you, God will deliver His people from bondage and pull them from the enemies' abyss. God, through Moses in the book of Exodus, delivered the children of Israel from their bondage in Egypt. You are seen as Moses of this century.

God will use you to deliver this generation of sinners from their sins through salvation. Yes, you are God's best friend, just like Abraham. Abraham sought and obeyed God; in return, God valued him, blessed him and called him His friend. God will hear you when you speak, especially if you honored Him.

The Scripture says in Job 22: 28 "You will also declare a thing, And it will be established for you; So light will shine on your ways." You are His ambassador through which He warns the humanity of the impending judgement on those who reject Christ as Lord and savior. No wonder He warns those who reject His offer of salvation in Christ Jesus saying, "He who rejects Me, and does not receive My words, has that which judges him—the word that I have spoken will judge him in the last day." John 12:48

The word "Rejection"

Rejection means:

- Dismissing.
- Refusal
- Turning down
- Declining.
- Turning away from God.

The above adjectives antagonize the word of God, and the general outcome is a sin against God. Have you ever been rejected before, if so, how do you feel? It takes the grace of God for us to hold our posture whenever we are rejected when we attempt to excuse someone to share the gospel of message. Rejection, in its totality, is outboast of the inner part of the devil's characteristics. Jesus Christ clearly stated in the above chapter and verse, "He that rejects me and receive not my word hath one that judge him, the word that I have spoken the same shall judge him on the last day."

I do not want to be rejected when I stand before God, and I believe that you, too, do not want to be rejected before Him. If you have the hope of eternal life then, trace your steps back to what God said to you, which you have brushed aside with some kind of excuses. Rejection of what God said carries a heavy weight of eternal punishment, which we know today as hellfire. Refusing to invite Jesus Christ into your life as Lord and personal savior results in eternal rejection. Rejection of God's commandments is not a good mark of a true Christian. God and his commandments should be the top priority of our life because no one has been able to do what He did for us. The only way to benefit from his unconditional love is to live a life as he desires, a Christ-like life. Secondly, He sacrificed His begotten Son, who died on the rugged cross to set us free from our sin. We are to seek Him and follow Him at all times. We are to be close to Him in every circumstance. The Bible said in Matthew 6:33, "But seek first the kingdom of God and His righteousness, and all these things shall be added to you."

Moses obeyed God, and God honored him before the Israelites. The Bible said the people see Moses as a god, and they followed and listened when he used to speak. They feared the wrath of God because of Moses as God's demonstrated his power through him. Moses is an example of someone you can define as "Man of God." God did mighty miracles through Moses as recorded in the book of Exodus, and finally, the Israelites were delivered from their bondage in Egypt. God accomplished His desire for His people through Moses. The same will happen to you. He will accomplish His desire through you in Jesus's name. "Believe on the Lord Jesus Christ, and you shall be saved. Have no other God beside Me.". Therefore, beloved, everything that you hold dear to yourself and are taking place of God in your life, are nothing but impediments to your relationship with God. Whatever it is, confess it before the Lord and turn away from it in Jesus's name. God will hear you and deliver you from it. He does not want any impediments to your spiritual life; rather, He wants you to overcome every obstacle and other forms of impediments in your spiritual life because He wants you to be free to worship Him in truth and in Spirit.

Moses followed God's specific instructions to deliver His people from bondage in Egypt, as a result of Moses obedience, God delivered His people, the Israelites from the hardship imposed on them by Pharaoh, king of Egypt. While Moses enjoyed the fruit of obedience, and was respected among the leaders in Israel and Egypt as well. Moses is a type of Jesus Christ in the Old Testament section of the Bible. His mission on earth was to deliver God's people from bondage. After the deliverance, I believe

Moses must have said in his mind, "It is finished.". Pharaoh has lost the battle. He saw the power of God in the demonstration. He saw the hand of God move against His enemies. He was the go-between" between God and the Israelites. He saw the children of Israel delivered from their slavery. Jesus was the "Go-between" God and humanity. He came to save man from the bondage of sin. When Jesus Christ was still on the cross, He saw the fulfillment of His mission. He endured to the last with His shed blood, and saw humanity being set free from the dominion of Satan, then He echoed, "It is finished." The question is, what has finished? The answer is the ultimate purpose for His coming to the earth was completely achieved, nothing was left undone. His death provided a way to heaven for the sinners. Our sins, which cause death, have been blotted out permanently. Satan has been stripped-off his pride and dominion over the people of God. Humanity, one more time, became God's own people. We all became sinless before God's eye. Your sins and mine were completely blotted out as a result of what Jesus did at the cross. Jesus Himself said, "I am the way, the truth, and the life. No one comes to the Father except through Me." John 14:6.

When Jesus was teaching His audience He specified to His audience His mission on earth. He said, "The Spirit of the Lord is upon Me, Because He has anointed Me To preach the gospel to the poor; He has sent Me [a]to heal the brokenhearted, To proclaim liberty to the captives and recovery of sight to the blind, To set at liberty those who are [b]oppressed;" Luke 4:18.

You and I are alive today as a result of what He did at the cross. During Moses's time, the law in effect was an "eye for an eye". There was no forgiveness unless animal sacrifices were presented to God; then He will cleanse the person-- this was a continuous process. In in other words, if the person does another sin, then he will have to come back to perform another animal sacrifice for forgiveness and for cleansing. But because God loves us so much, He sent Jesus to the earth to die one-time death shedding his blood once for humanity. John 3:16 says, "For God so loved the world that He gave His only begotten Son, that whoever believes in Him should not perish but have everlasting life." His death is the only way through which we are saved. It is by His Grace we are saved, now our work here is to follow through His words to save ourselves from hellfire as there is no other way. Ephesians 2:8 says, "For by grace you have been saved through faith, and that not of yourselves; it is the gift of God." So Moses served the Lord under the law, but Jesus Christ brought grace. Today you and I are under the grace of God;, that is why it is absolutely necessary to invite Jesus by faith into your heart as Lord and savior. Grace is God's unmerited favor on us otherwise humankind would have suffered from eternal damnation because of our sins. We all are supposed to die and go to hell, but God had mercy on us and sent Jesus Christ to die on our behalf and rose again because He is not a man but God.

Beloved of God, the big question remains to be answered, and that is, are you saved by Grace alone or by works? We are saved by Grace alone and not by works. It needs to be taught more clearly and explained in our different congregations for many do not understand the difference between grace and works. As a result of this lack of knowledge in these terms, many people in our congregation depend entirely on their physical presence and works they do in the church and for the church to earn them eternal life. What a spiritual misguidedness!

Grace and works explained.
Works

Works' is pivotal for belief in God. In fact, without works, the ministry will not be able to accomplish the purpose for which it exists. For works to be valued in the service to our God, it must be accompanied with faith in the risen savior Jesus Christ. The Scripture says, "Faith without works is dead." In other words, if you have faith in God to win a soul for the kingdom of God, it requires you to step out of your comfort zone and go witnessing and sharing the message of gospel to the unbelievers. God promised Abraham a son and that He will be a father of nations. Remember Abraham had no child. How could this promise be accomplished? Abraham had faith in God for the promise to come true. To accomplish the promise:

1. He believed God's word for him.

2. He did the works by Holy matrimonial relationship with his wife Sarah, resulting in the birth of Isaac. (Son of promise).

God's part is to speak the word, and our part is to receive it and apply our faith, then only the manifestation will be evident.

Faith in Jesus Christ + zero = eternal life
Works + church attendance -Christ = Hell fire.
Everything you do to earn eternal life - Jesus Christ = to hell fire.

As we have already seen above, works must be complemented by faith in order to have value. Also, faith must agree with works to receive whatever God promised you and for God to meet your expectations. God has His part to fulfill, and you have your part to fulfill. Most times, our expeditions are delayed because we did not do our part. Always endeavor to find out your responsibility when you are expecting from God.

Grace

Theologically, Grace is God's intervention to rescue sinners from the penalty of their sins. Grace means God's sending of His only begotten Son Jesus Christ to Hell via the cross to rescue and recover all that Satan has stolen from humanity. 2nd Corinthians 5:21 says, "For He made Him who knew no sin to be sin for us, that we might become the righteousness of God in Him." The Bible defines Grace as unmerited favor. We have all received good things from God, yes we have, look at yourself and family. In view of man's pitiful condition, we are in no way qualified to receive any good thing from Him. Romans 3:23 declared that all have sinned and fall short of the glory of God. Yes, we have, but God loves us so much He did not want us to die in our sins. Therefore, He took the most painful and worst pattern to save us because death was a prerequisite to set humanity free from the grip of Satan. As His grace stepped in to save us, He let His only begotten Son to be killed on the cross. Ephesians 2:8-9 says, "For by grace you have been saved through faith, and that not of yourselves; it is the gift of God, 9 not of works, lest anyone should boast."

We are all enjoying God's grace. God's grace is evident in our daily lives that we are saved and being saved daily. His grace is always available as we wake up daily to depend on Him. His grace leads us for the rest of the day, and enables us to overcome the obstacles and challenges of our daily life. It is because of His grace that you and I are still living. God's grace is born out of His love for humanity. The scripture says, "God is love and love is God." Love cannot be separated from God, and so God cannot be separated from love. That is why He relates to us in love. His grace is the good news we have today. Are you experiencing the grace of God? Grace also can be defined as the righteousness of God given through faith in Jesus Christ. After my daily prayer, my family always end the section by saying the grace: May the grace of our Lord Jesus Christ, the love of God, and the fellowship of the Holy Spirit rest and abide with us now and forevermore in Jesus Christ Mighty name, Amen. May this grace be with you and guide you as you search For Him through the pages of this book.

CHAPTER 6

Case Study Five: Elijah

Elijah, the Tishbite from the region of Gilead, was one the two men mentioned in the Scripture who did not die but was taken up to the sky. He had extraordinary benefit of experiencing rapture as a result of his complete obedience and confident in God. Elijah obeyed every single word the Lord had said to him. He was seen as one the most powerful prophets of most high God during his time, powerful because he carried out God's instructions as he received it. He obeyed every single word of God.

He carried out specific instructions to root out sins and ungodliness in the midst of the people of God. One of the instructions to Elijah as recorded in the Bible says. "Arise, go up to meet the messengers of the king of Samaria, and say to them, 'Is it because there is no God in Israel that you are going to inquire of Baal-Zebub, the god of Ekron?" 2 King 1:3

Elijah featured during the reign of wicked King Herod and his wife, Jezebel. He was the most confrontational prophet ever lived. "As the Lord God of Israel lives, before whom I stand, there shall not be dew nor rain these years, except at my word." 1 King 17:1.

Elijah's various kinds of ways of delivering God's word to the people in different settings resulted to people turning away from sin to seeking God of heaven and earth. He was so dedicated to carrying out what God said that whenever he entered a city people began to tremble because he always come with a message from the God, the message may be for rebuke, correction or instant judgement of Idol worshipers.

Elijah dedicated to carrying out what God said to him without any forms of adulterations or arguments with God or his audience. You see God commuted the gospel into our hands to preach and defend it. Every true believer of Jesus Christ is an apologetic, i.e. to defend the gospel. Our mode of defense is not with gun and knife, it is not by killing others but by loving people, this is why the gospel of Jesus is called the gospel of love. What you preach to the world is love. God is Love and Love is God. (1 John 4:8) Jesus Christ is love; He is the word of God, the gospel we preach to the world today. Are you preaching and defending this gospel as the Lord directed? In one way or the other, you must be sharing this gospel of Love. If you are not sharing the gospel, it will be accounted to you as disobedience. Telling other people about the gospel of Jesus with the intention of encouraging them to invite Jesus Christ into their life as lord and savior is the primary reason for the church's existence. You and I are witnesses for Jesus Christ. A witness is one who sees an invent take place. We have personally experience the touch of Jesus. The Holy Spirit had revealed Christ and what He did in our hearts. His touch is our testimony to the world. He changed us and gave a new life in Him.

Lessons from Prophet Elijah

1. Prophet Elijah knew what God said to him, and he obeyed and declared it to the people. As a result of his obedience, sin was eradicated from the land and the people worshipped their God.
2. Prophet Elijah's crusade whereby the prophets of Baal and other Baal sympathizers were invited which marked the beginning of the end of the worship of Ball in Israel. Elijah proclaimed the truth of the word of God to the people with evidence of God's presence to consume the sacrifice brought about repentance. The Lord is God! The Lord is God; they cried.
3. Even though there was sin in the land, yet there were people who lived in obedience to the word of God. Are you one of those the Lord is referring to when He said to Elijah, "there are ten

thousand people who have not bow down to Baal idol?" We have all witnessed a lot of events that seems to derail our faith in only one true God, events like mysterious advancement in technology. In our world today, people no longer go to the church; rather, they prefer to stay home and glued to the TV for worship. It is not common to see people going to the church with their Bible. The World is in competition with the church, which has resulted in significant influence on the church in its stand in faith in Christ Jesus.

4. Boldness.

As already mentioned, Elijah was the greatest confrontational prophet in the Bible. He was known as a bold and no-nonsense type of man of God. He delivered the word of God as it is. God judged those who refused to repent from Elijah's message of salvation. He Judged Ahab and Jezebel, and the Baal worshipers leading to the slaughtering of 450 prophets of Baal. God rewards those who listened and did what Elijah asked of them, like the woman at Zarephath.

We like Elijah are to be bold in delivering the message of salvation to the world. Salvation in Jesus Christ is what the world need to stand and survive. Everyday people refuse to accept Jesus Christ as their Lord and Savior, for whom God's only intention is to live and prosper, but their refusal leads to hellfire. Whenever someone dies in sin, then the purpose of God for that individual was not achieved and it grieves God to heart. Therefore beloved, to deliver this message, you and I need boldness just like Elijah. The scripture said, "For God has not given us a spirit of fear, but of power and of love and of a sound mind." 2 Timothy 1:7.

Yes beloved, you have the power of God living inside of you ready to be used in every circumstance of need. Again in 1 John 4:4, "You are of God, little children, and have overcome them, because He who is in you is greater than he who is in the world." The knowledge of the word of God helps to motivate you and guarantee the benefits you have in the Lord as His child. Those benefits, including His anointing, has God given to you for His service.

5. Relationship:

It is a state of been connected with someone or something. We all are separated from God as a result of sin of Adam. But, God loves us unconditionally, and decided to bring us back to Himself. He blessed us with His mercy and love so that we could have a close relationship with Him. The reason why He gave His only begotten Son to die on the cross was to bring us close to Him. So, to have a close relationship with God, you must invite Jesus Christ into your life as Lord and savior by faith. Faith in Him alone will create unshakable and unbreakable relationship with Him. As many that who received Him as their God and Savior, He gave them the right to become the children of God. John 1:12

A genuine relationship with Him will give you access to His power and anointing. These essentials are necessary for you to fulfill your ministry. You can never be an obedient servant of God without His Spirit indwelling you. He helps you live a Christian lifestyle and practice how to live righteously for Jesus Christ. He will equip you and direct you to live word to word for Jesus and focus on fulfilling the calling you received from Him. Paul spoke in this line to Timothy and said: "But you be watchful in all things, endure afflictions, do the work of an evangelist, fulfill your ministry." 2 Timothy 4:5. If God calls you, He will make sure that you are equipped for service. Again in Jeremiah God made it even clearer:

"Before I formed you in the womb I knew you; before you were born I sanctified you; I ordained you a prophet to the nations." Jeremiah 1:5.

We all should accept the fact that we have already been prepared for the service of the Lord. According to the Jeremiah, God Himself has ordained you as one of His servants. If you acknowledge this fact that you have been ordained, then you are to look for who ordained you and follow the instructions thereafter-- ordained means to confer holy orders, to consecrate, or to install. You are to live in a certain strict way and not to live or follow any other person. You have the order to follow.

Seek Him

The scripture says, If you seek Him you will find Him if you seek Him with all your heart. You seek the Lord from:

a. All the pages of the Bible. Study the Bible day and night.
b. Obey all that He said in the Bible and apply what He said in your life.
c. Attend Bible believing congregations to hear the word of God.
d. Acknowledge the presence of the indwelling Holy Spirit in your life and listen to Him. The Holy Spirit will reveal and teach you all you suppose to know about your God. God is willing to reveal Himself to you so that you can be able to tell others about Him. He created you with the purpose to expand his kingdom. As you start doing something for the kingdom of God, He sees you and blesses you to a greater height in your spiritual journey.
e. When Paul and his team was on the road to Damascus to persecute Christians, Jesus met him. After Jesus had introduced himself to him, He told Paul what to do, I mean the next step into fulfilling his ministry. "Arise and go into the city, and you will be told what you must do." Act 9:6.

There are some responsibilities God has assigned for you to do and He has been talking to you about. We are alive because you and I have not finished our assignments here on this earth. Your assignment is clearly written in the Bible, the Word of God. Again, Apostle Paul clearly stated in 2 Corinthians 5:17:

"Therefore, if anyone is in Christ, he is a new creation; old things have passed away; behold, all things have become new." 2 Corinthians 5:17.

Every single Christian in the Church should see themselves as ambassador for Christ. Do you see yourself as one?

The word ambassador is the highest-ranking representative to a specific nation or international organization abroad. As an ambassador of the Lord, your main assignment is to communicate the message of God to the people on the earth. In specific terms, it is to relate the mind of God to His people (the world) to receive instructions from Him and apply it to different life aspects. God wants you to reach out to the world with His message of love, "For God so loved the world that He gave His only begotten Son Jesus Christ that whosoever believe in Him should not perish but have everlasting life." John 3:16. God's ultimate intention is to save you and to give you eternal life!

Whenever you win a person to the Lord and the heaven gets the signal from the earth that someone has given his/ her life over to Jesus Christ, there is always rejoice and jubilations. The heaven rejoices because a sinner has been saved from Hellfire and a soul has been added to the kingdom of God. God wins when a person receives Chris as Lord and savior. Yes, do you want the heavens to rejoice for your service for the Lord? Then evangelize and win souls. Will you start doing that today? God calls you and responds to you in the time of need when you get into the art of telling people about His love. The scripture says,

"How beautiful upon the mountains are the feet of him who brings good news, Who proclaims peace, Who brings glad tidings of good things, Who proclaims salvation, Who says to Zion, "Your God reigns!"" Isaiah 52:7.

Samuel.

Samuel was also one of the greatest prophets of God we read in the Bible. God called Samuel at a very young age while he was still serving Eli. At that time, Samuel was not able to distinguish between God's voice and his master Eli the Priest until Eli instructed him on what to answer. Evidently, God spoke again, and by following the instructions of Eli, he was able to communicate with God. Samuel answered, "Speak for your servant is listening".

What God said to Samuel: 1 Samuel 3:11

"See I am about to do something in Israel that will make the ears of every one who hears about it tingle. At that time I will carry out against Eli everything I spoke against his family."

What God said to Samuel was a clear instruction of purpose. It was supposed to be delivered to the person it was meant for. Some times what God said to us may not necessarily be for someone else, it might be for your own good. The word of God in the Bible spoke to the church; it is an instruction on how to live to please God. Timothy puts it this way, "All Scripture is given by inspiration of God, and is profitable for doctrine, for reproof, for correction, for [a]instruction in righteousness. " 2 Timothy 3:16.

No wonder when one first comes to Christ emphasis are mostly laid on studying the word of God Day and night. Doing this will help you know Him better, and your faith will increase as well. It will also help you to know when He speaks to you. God wants you to know Him and His ways so that you can build a strong relationship with Him. God wants us to understand that He lives inside of each and every one of His children.

Like Elijah, Samuel was a well-respected servant of God. He was known and feared because of his radical approach in obedience to what God said to him. He carried out God's instructions without fear or feeling of what the people might think of Him. Samuel carried out what we may see as a difficult task. When the Israelite wanted a king contrary to God's design for them, He sent Samuel to anoint Saul, the son of Kish, the king to be. It will not be an overstatement to say that Samuel and king Soul lived in a difficult period in Israel. The Philippians were constantly harassing the armies of Israel.

When God rejected Saul from been the king of Israel, He sent Samuel to take the message of rejection to Saul. Samuel delivered the message as is, no alteration of the exact message God sent. Samuel hated what God hated and loved what God loved. He condemned what God condemned. He lived his life to the service of God and spoke against the evil of the day and brought revival to the people of Israel. God called you and me to carry His message of reconciliation to the world. As already said, He ordained you for this reason like Samuel, and we are to deliver it as is. It is erroneous to alter God's message. However, if anyone modifies it, God will add to him the plagues described in this book. "For I testify to everyone who hears the words of the prophecy of this book: If anyone adds to these things, God will add to him the plagues that are written in this book; and if anyone takes away from the words of the book of this prophecy, God shall take away his part from the Book of Life, from the holy city, and from the things which are written in this book." Revelation 22:18-19.

Again Jesus Christ in one of His teachings said to His disciples, "Remember the word that I said to you, 'A servant is not greater than his master.' If they persecuted Me, they will also persecute you. If they kept My word, they will keep yours also." John 15:20.

Lessons from Prophet Samuel.

1. Mother's prayer: One significant lesson to learn from Samuel's intimacy with God is his mother's ceaseless prayer to God for her son Samuel. Hannah was barren, but she prayed, requesting a son from God. God answered the prayer.
2. The birth of Samuel: At a young age, Hannah took him to the house of God in the care of Eli, the priest. Thereby fulfilling her promise to God by giving the child back to Him. I believe Hannah must have told Samuel the story of his birth. God expects every parent to pray for his/her children regularly. He wants us to train them in the way of the Lord, to serve Him. The Bible clearly stated, "Train a child in the way he should go, and when he grows up, he will not depart from it." Have you introduced your children to God? Do you pray for your children? God is interested in your children; that is why God commanded: "Leave little children to come to me." Hannah taught us to pray as she prayed her son into obedience. Samuel sought for God because his mother sought for God.

3. Obedience: Samuel obeyed every word of his mom when she took him to the house of God to live Eli, the priest who he did not know or was familiar with. Yet, he did not refuse or resist but obeyed his mother. When God spoke to Saul through Samuel, and Samuel disobeyed, Samuel made a statement to Saul saying: "To obey is better than sacrifice." Samuel also obeyed Eli the priest while his children sinned against the Almighty God, but Samuel obeyed God. He took what God said to him and applied it to where God wanted it to be delivered.

4. Samuel respected and honored the Lord through obedience and service, while the sons of Eli dishonored the Lord by not been faithful to the Him. They also despised the offering with contempt.

5. Samuel willingly sought the Lord until he recognized God's call upon his life. In 1 Samuel 3:7, it is stated that Samuel loved the Lord so much that he chose to sleep in the house of the Lord instead of the Eli's house, which I believe must be a more comfortable place to sleep.

6. The Bible said that the word from God was rare in those days, and visions were infrequent. 1 Samuel 3:1: But Samuel heard the word of God and responded with enthusiasm. Have you done so recently? Beloved God said something to you and He is waiting for a response.

Sin was the ultimate reason why they were not able to get a word from God. They resisted God's presence in their hearts, everyone did what pleased them. Beloved if you can compare those days and today, you will categorically discover that our generation has resisted God more even in this period of grace in the history of the world. Grace period is a season in which we enjoy God's blessing without actually working for it. The grace of God sets in to help us when we are weak in our faith. Today, there is a gravitation of the world's ethics into our congregations; the church is in pitiful conditions, so God's Grace sets in to carry us through. Do you recognize this in your life? Our church buildings are gradually growing into emptiness. People no longer go to fellowship with one another despite the fact that God commands us not to avoid the assembly of one another. The population of Christian who chooses to worship via the television are increasing as days go by. My wife Helen and I talked about these issues with concern. We have seen and heard that in some nations, many places of worship (church buildings) are virtually empty, and a post read "For sale" sign posted in front of it.

I said to my wife, Helen, God knows all this and reacted positively. When the time comes, the word of God will hold true as He said, "No gate of hell shall prevail the church from marching on." The time is near when people will worship God in truth and Spirit. I reminded her about September 11, 2001, in America when the terrorists rammed a passenger plane into the World Trade Center, people were scared and looking for escape. The evil of that September 2001 demonstrated why an enlightened nation like the US would suffer this tragedy. After that event, many people ran to God confessing their sins, those who believed were saved.

Every church building was filled to the brim with people searching for God to intervene, and as time elapsed, people began to forget the event of Sept. 11. They must have heard the truth of the word of God preached to them at that time, I believe. I sincerely believe that God will do something to help America.

We are living to acknowledge His presence in us as He calls us every day for His fellowship. We are not going to make the blood He shed for humanity of no -effect.

Samuel fulfilled his ministry

Samuel focused on fulfilling what God said to him. He delivered the word of God as he heard from God while fulfilling his ministry. Apostle spoke to Timothy, encouraging him to fulfill his Ministry. Have you thought in this direction? God desired that we fulfill our calling before our time on earth runs out. Friend, we continue to live because we have work to do and our ministry to fulfill. Paul speaking to his audience, stated, "To live is Christ, to die is gain." In other words, he meant as long as he lives, he will do what God said. Evidently, if he were to die, he will surely be with Jesus Christ. Your desire and mine are to be with Jesus Christ after we die.

In addition to Samuel's accomplishments, he trained prophets who served the Lord with great respect and enthusiasm. Samuel brought in what we know today as kingdom soul multiplication as his school of prophets produced maximum kingdom-minded citizens. He is God's right-hand man when it comes to obedience. He judged Israel for many years and was the last Judge in Israel before the kings began to rule. He anointed the two kings chosen by God (Saul and David), which gives him crucial importance in Israelites history. He was considered the greatest Judge. He took his assignment from God very seriously. In reciprocal direction, God answered all his prayers.

We see from the life of Samuel that he chose to believe God and do all that God said to him. In return, God honored him before the people of Israel. He was respected and lived a godly lifestyle. All the prayers he tabled before God received immediate answers.

The scripture declares in Acts 10:34; "Then Peter opened his mouth and said: "In truth I perceive that God shows no partiality." God who walked with Samuel, is the same in existence today. He will walk with you if you let Him. He is available 24/7, the only thing you need to do is to invite His son by faith into your life as Lord and savior, then ask Him what He wants you to do, and you will get your answer. Obedience to Him builds up trust, once He trusts you He will walk with you. Samuel was bold and fearless, the key verse in the Bible, which portrays his willingness to serve the Almighty, also builds confidence in the life of believers. His word to King Saul:

"Has the Lord as great delight in burnt offerings and sacrifices as in obeying the voice of the Lord? Behold, to obey is better than sacrifice, and to heed than the fat of rams. For rebellion is as the sin of witchcraft, and stubbornness is as iniquity and idolatry. Because you have rejected the word of the Lord, He also has rejected you from being king." 1 Samuel 15: 22-23.

God said to us to take the good news and message of salvation to the world of sinners, from where we were delivered. Read my other books on how you can share what God said to you with the sole aim of bringing them to the Lord. Not only does God want to save us, but He also wants to have an intimate relationship with us. That is why he indwells by His Spirit.

Intimacy with God.

The intimate relationship with God starts with:

1. Inviting Jesus Christ into your life as Lord and savior.
2. Studying the word of God in the Holy Bible daily.
3. Applying what His Word said to you in your daily orientations.
4. Sharing your day to day experience with other people.
5. Fellowship with one another and attending the gathering of His people on Sundays.
6. Practicing to live for Him alone.
7. Always appreciate what Jesus Christ did for you and the rest of humanity.
8. Practicing to relate to the indwelling presence of the Holy Spirit in you. Talk to him, tell him your mind, and wait for the answer.
9. Loving the Lord and His people with all your heart.
10. Reaching out with the spiritual and physical needs of His people.

CHAPTER 7

Case Study Six: Jeremiah

Jeremiah is one of the most popular prophets of God in the Old Testament. He was from Judah province and received his calling from God to the seat of a prophet. He received the revelation from God that God knows him from his mother's womb and ordained him to the position of a prophet. Jeremiah 1:5 says:

"Before I formed you in the womb I knew you; Before you were born I sanctified[a] you; I ordained you a prophet to the nations."

This statement of facts says much about you and the message God gave to us. God was the one who allowed you to be conceived. God chose you to be born and gave you life, up to this day. God made you and cared for you when you were in the womb and brought you to the earth through the process of conception. God loves you just as you are because you represent His glory. He sent you and me to His world for the same purpose He sent Jeremiah-- solely for the salvation of God's people. Jeremiah lived during the time when the worship of Idol was common in In Israel. Throughout the period of Jeremiah's prophetic office, He did what God said to him, and was totally committed to doing what God said.

He was known because of his steadfastness in taking what God said to the people of God. He preached the word with what I call 'holy anger.' He hated sin just as God hates sins. He sees God's need to deliver His people, so he runs with what God said and delivered it the dying nations of God's people. He was seen as a preaching prophet. He condemned Idolatry and the categories of false prophets and priests during his lifetime. As a result of the difficulties, he went to Biblical scholars who studied the book of Jeremiah referred him as "the weeping prophet" He wept for sins of the people.

Primarily he was the last of prophets who were sent by God to the southern kingdom, which comprises of Judah and Benjamin. God repeatedly warned them, but they would not listen. So God called and ordained Jeremiah for this specific message and commanded them to turn away from the worship of Idol.

In comparison to our world today you wouldn't have to go far to observe the similarities between people of today's world ad people of Jeremiah's rime You and I are living in a world where the worship of Idol is practiced and conduction daily. There are many buildings in our communities and town designated as house of worship but are a place where Satan and his cohorts are worshiped. One of which is located in the USA called the church of Satan in the USA. It has branches all over the USA and other parts of the world. Consequently, anything that has more preference and priority in your life than God is of course an Idol-- God sees it so. Your wife, money, job, family can stand as Idol if you are not careful. I love my wife and my children but not more than God. I let them know that they are not first in my life, "God is" I let them also know that I shouldn't be first in their life, but God should. We all have this understanding.

Theologically, Idol is anything that you put first in your life or anything you love more than God. The Scripture says, "You shall not make for yourself a carved image—any likeness of anything that is in heaven above, or that is in the earth beneath, or that is in the water under the earth." Exodus 20:4.

As already discussed anything you put above God in your life is Idol, and God does not like it. A lot of people worship Idol unknowingly, which is why you should search the Scripture daily and fellowship with people of the same faith.

God is a jealous God

"For you shall worship no other god, for the Lord, whose name is Jealous, is a jealous God." Exodus34:14.

One of the characteristics of God is His jealous nature; that is why He is called in the Scripture, "jealous God."

The relationship between God and people is mirrored in the symbolism of marriage. Relationship with the Almighty God is a long time covenant, just like married couple that pledges death till we part. If the relationship between the couple is based on true love, none of them would be attracted to someone else or violate the marriage pledge.. The strong ties, therefore, attract jealousy if one has a commitment elsewhere.

God is jealous of us because He does not want to share us with any other entity and wants us by Himself. Failure to put Him first attracts His wrath in a very devastating manner.

Jeremiah 3:6-8 says, "Have you seen what backsliding Israel has done? She has gone up on every high mountain and under every green tree, and there played the harlot. And I said, after she had done all these things, 'Return to Me.' But she did not return. And her treacherous sister Judah saw it. Then I saw that for all the causes for which backsliding Israel had committed adultery, I had put her away and given her a certificate of divorce; yet her treacherous sister Judah did not fear, but went and played the harlot also."

When we give ourselves to the Lord, we will be in the position to hear Him and carry out the commandments as He needed it done

Every word of God written in the Bible is to be heard and obeyed. In fact, God evaluates the love we have for Him by our obedience.

Proverb 7:2 says, "Keep my commands and live, and my law as the apple of your eye." The word of God is the only key to living because God lives inside of you and directs your lives.

You are alive and active today, not because of your hard work or because you have a good health care provider. You are alive because God has some assignments for you. The calling of God on anyone is for a purpose. That is why His grace overshadows you daily, keeping you in shape to finish what He wants you to do. God never does a thing without a reason, and you are where you are for a reason.

Practical lessons from the life of Prophet Jeremiah.

1. Believe in God

Jeremiah's visceral understanding of the fact that mankind cannot live a fulfilling life without the guidance and the direction of the Holy Spirit. "Oh Lord, I know that the way of the man is not in himself; it is not in man who walks to direct his own steps." Jeremiah 10:23. Jeremiah knew from his interactions with God that man could not survive on this earth without God. God is the source of life through which all things thrive.

Another supporting passage says, "Cursed is the man who trusts in man and makes flesh his strength whose heart departs from the Lord." Jeremiah 17:5.

2. Relationship

Jeremiah has a very good relationship with God. It was when God called Jeremiah and introduced Himself that he actually began to know Him. He developed faith in Him over time. His knowledge of God led him to cry and condemn sin of the people. He was totally overwhelmed by God's presence. As he discovered the omnipotence of God, he declared in one of his consultations with God in prayer, "Ah Lord God! Behold, you have made the heavens and the earth by your great power and outstretched arm. There is nothing too hard for you." Jeremiah 32:17. As we walk with the

Lord, we are to communicate with Him in every way we can; we are to speak our mind to Him, leaving nothing hidden, just as you talk to your dad. God doesn't like it when we distance ourselves. He wants to be part of everyday activity and life aspect. We can start today to practice His presence and to recognize His voice. Beloved knowing God intimately is achievable by:

a) Reading and studying the Bible (word of God) daily. When you do this, God talks to you directly through His written words.

b) Pray at all times. Develop the habit of praying daily, whether you have reason to pray or not. First Thessalonians 5:16-18 states that pray without ceasing, "Rejoice always, pray without ceasing, in everything give thanks; for this is the will of God in Christ Jesus for you."

c) Practice living what your God said to you in the Bible.

d) Focus your mind always on Jesus Christ, bearing on your mind the sacrifice He offered for you on the cross.

e) Seek and recognize the presence of the Holy Spirit participation in your daily work. Always listen to the still small voice as He directs you on the right path whenever you make a decision.

As Jeremiah came to know the Lord, he never relented in his service to Him, with this closeness, intimacy was achieved. Then he was able to:

a) Proclaim the word of God with boldness and power.

b) He was not scared or afraid of the ruling authority of that time.

c) He saw the power of God in demonstration and received answers to his request to God.

God confirmed His words spoken from Jeremiah. He condemned sins of all types and lifted the name of God on high.

Jeremiah encountered and had a dialogue with God, and perhaps that was the defining moment when Jeremiah came to believe in God intimately. He heard what God said to him then he began to act on it. All of Jeremiah's actions were based on what God said to him. His messages were related to doom because of the disobedience of the people of the time. God was very direct to Jeremiah as He gave him instructions and revealed His intending action against sin. The same God who spoke to Jeremiah is the same God we worship and will be the same God our future generations will worship. He is the same God who said to Moses, "I am that I am" say to the people May I ask you what your relationship with God is? Is He God to you, or is he god to you? How do you see Him in your everyday living?

4.   Jeremiah hated sin.

We all carry the sins we inherited from Adam and Eve. The Bible says that we have all sinned and fallen short of the glory of God. Romans 3:23. Jeremiah repented from his sins and hated sins from that time. He cried for the sins of the people and reached out to them with the word of God for repentance. He actually wept for the sins of the people. Probably that is why he is referred to as the "weeping prophet." Are you sorry for the sins you committed and have you repented from it all? Have you gone back to God after your sins drove you away from Him? For us to be right with God, we are to repent from our sins and accept God's offer of forgiveness in the person of Jesus Christ.

He assured us in 1 John 1:9 if we confess our sins He is faithful and just to forgive us from our sins and to cleanse us from all unrighteousness.

What God wants us to do?

When you discover through the word of God that you are elected as one of His ambassadors, what you do from that moment is of utmost importance to God and you as well. God's desire is for you to obey Him in all things. He wants you to discover who He is:

1.   He wants you and me to believe and trust Him in everything and in all things we do.
2.   He wants to reveal to us some specific things about eternal life and how to get there.
3.   He wants us to know Him and to know for sure that He is with us at all times. God does not want us to see Him as a distant God

of whom, if we don't go to a certain place to pray, He will not hear us. He wants us to know that He is always by our side and ready to bless us and save us when we call on Him. Knowing God and knowing Him intimately begins right after we give our life to the Lord Jesus Christ as Lord and savior. When you willingly give your life over to Jesus Christ, you have obeyed God's greatest commandment. You have made God your father. You become a child of God, according to John 1:12. He now indwells you by His Spirit and will never leave you. He takes a residence in you and makes decisions for you. Joshua saw the goodness of the Lord and His love was reported in Joshua 24:15 as, "As for me and my House, we will serve the Lord."

We like Jeremiah are to stand for the Lord's cause. We are to stand strong and never shaken. You and I are given the authority to speak the word of God, especially in the area of Evangelism and other situations of need. The Scripture reminds us, "Behold, I give you the authority to trample on serpents and scorpions, and over all the power of the enemy, and nothing shall by any means hurt you." Luke 10:19.We are to serve the Lord with all our hearts and strength and with everything in our possession. When was the last time you shared the gospel with someone else? Did you think about sharing the gospel with others or encouraging those who do?

CHAPTER 8

Case Study Seven: Prophet Isaiah

Prophet Isaiah is one of the popular prophets of God both in the Old Testament and the New Testament. He was popular because of his uncompromising approach in delivering what God said to him to the Israelites. Isaiah delivered what he heard from God with zero adulteration. He convicted the people of sins and reminded of God's punishment, including eternal damnation for disobedience.

Isaiah's prophecies which he received from God, were fulfilled. He prophesied the birth of Jesus Christ and His deity nature.

Therefore the Lord Himself will give you a sign: The virgin will conceive and give birth to a son, and will call Him Immanuel (which means God with us).

We all are living witnesses of the truth in the word of God, which the Holy Spirit revealed to us individually-- the reality of the birth, death and resurrection of Jesus Christ. The key to receive God's revelation in our heart is "TO BELIEVE". To believe is to accept as truth, or to have confidence in what God said to you. Jesus spoke to one of His audience, saying, "If only you believe you will see the glory of God." John11:40. Not only did God expects us to believe and trust Him in all things, but also to believe Him in His words. The word of God declares, "And He is before all things, and in Him all things consist." Colossians 1:17.

The whole world is held together by this ultimate truth of the word of God. God's love is seen in the death and resurrection of Jesus Christ. The scripture informs us that "For in Him dwells all the fullness of the Godhead bodily." Colossians 2:9

Isaiah decided to run with what God said to him and to bring the message of salvation to the people of Judah. God constantly reaches out to us in love to deliver, forgive and restore the relationship which was lost at the Garden of Eden; as a result of sin. How will you feel when you realize that God loves you and has forgiven all the sins you ever committed? Incidentally, Isaiah's name means Salvation, so his name follows him. No wonder he preached the message of salvation to the people. He prophesied the second coming of Jesus Chris, Isaiah 40:3-5. Today, Christian's faith looks forward to the second coming of Jesus Christ. Other biblical passages also discuss the second coming, such as Matthew 24. Revelation.

Lessons from prophet Isaiah.

Isaiah loved God and was determined to serve him. He wrote his prophecies in a book according to God's direction and preached repentance from evil. He revealed God's unchangeable character and, at the same time, inform the Israelites that God will hold them responsible for their sins. Matthew quoted Isaiah's prophecies when he was describing John the Baptist ministry in Matthew 3:3 and Isaiah 40:3.

It was the love he had for God that motivated him to run with the vision he got from God. Isaiah was also a preaching prophet. He preached to his audience the message of conviction, repentance, and seeking God with all their heart. In our generation, the key message we preach today is repentance from sin and inviting Jesus Christ into our lives as Lord and savior. As we make this commitment, God expects us to engage in massive soul winning so that others who do not know Him will come to Him by faith and be saved. Part of the massive Evangelism is writing about Him with the intention that people will read about Him and gave their life over to Jesus. Isaiah's book was written well over 2500 years ago, and the book is still relevant today, ministering to millions of people to lead a life of faith in Jesus Christ. The wisdom of God, which is clearly seen in Isaiah's writing, shows mercy and love of God to humanity. Isaiah encouraging his audience said, "To the law and to the testimony! If they do not speak according to this word, it is because there is no light in them." Isaiah 8:20.

Who do you trust?

"In the year that King Uzziah died, I saw also the Lord sitting upon a throne, high and lifted up, and his train filled the temple." Isaiah 6:1.

From Isaiah, chapter 1:6 following clearly showed that Prophet Isaiah has some level of comfort with King Uzziah. It was after the death of King Uzziah that Isaiah actually discovered the calling of the Lord upon His life. He was able to see the need to answer the calling of God on him. God took the opportunity to reveal to Isaiah his heart and the hearts of man. I believed that Isaiah was looking up to the king instead of God from the Isaiah chapter one proved that Isaiah had the general knowledge of God. He had not come to personal relationship with Him; if he had, then, he was not serious in seeking Him. He was an ordinary church-goer. Beloved, I tried to figure out why Isaiah waited until the king demise before he was able to seek the Lord? I do feel that Isaiah has some sort of emotional distress and lack of peace; thereby, he ran to the Lord for help. When God took the king away then only Isaiah discovers who God is and the calling of God upon his life.

Beloved, we all have some personal issues that seem to hinder our search and worship of God. My focus to do what God had intended for me was hampered, thereby making me less effective in my calling. Ken was my younger brother. I did not know how much I love my brother until he passed away. I felt stripped of all I had until I had the inner witness of the Holy Spirit, leading me to do what He called me to do. It was that my dreams of service for God met its realization. It was then I completed my degrees in preparation for the service of God. It was then I become an author of many Christian books for Evangelism. It was then I become even more serious in serving the Lord as His grace abides.

If you are not serving the Lord or you discover hindering the relationship between you and God, it is your responsibility to identify such things and present it to God. God wants total worship, and you are the one to identify why you are not growing spiritually.

Your job as "I am" may be the problem.

Your children,

Your friends,

Your title or position in life,

Your education,

Your emotional condition, and

Pride of life.

Or maybe you are satisfied with the level of relationship you have with Him. Find out what is slowing or interfering with your growth in the Lord.

When King Uzziah died, God opened Isaiah eyes to see what was standing on his way of spiritual growth. Isaiah saw his and other people's sinful actions. Isaiah believed what God revealed to him and cried, "Woe is me, for I am undone! Because I am a man of unclean lips, and I dwell in the midst of a people of unclean lips; for my eyes have seen the King, the Lord of hosts." Isaiah 6:5.

When you deal with what is standing between you and God, then you will be able to know the Lord and the purpose of your calling, only then you will walk in it. God wants you to grow in His knowledge.

He does not want you to be stagnant in your present spiritual life. Isaiah discovered man's sinful nature and was terrified of how much we have all failed.

He realized that we have all sinned against Holy God. (Romans 3:23) He knew that repentance and seeking God is the key for reconciliation.

Isaiah realized that he and the rest of the world have sinned and so he began to reach out to the world for repentance.

He saw the holiness of God dealing with sinful people and was terrified man's woe condition.

In the past, God spoke to our ancestors through the prophets at many times and in various ways, but in these last days he has spoken to us by his son, who he appointed heir of all things, and through whom also he made the universe; Hebrew 1:1-2.

Ever since the creation of the world, God has been using various ways to communicate with humanity in the most meaningful way. He spoke to those who have lived and passed. He spoke to Adam and Eve on specific terms; what to do and live. He tested them in the area of obedience in which they failed. "The day you eat of the tree I told you not to eat you shall surely die." As already stated, He spoke to the prophets and other various ways to communicate His love to humanity.

Reasons God Spoke to you.

1.   Love. God wants to tell us that He loves us these He expressed in the pages of the Bible. John3:16

If you love someone, you will always like to talk to that person. You will like to spend time with him. True love creates intimacy. You can do everything, including giving your life for the person. God expressed His love for humanity by sending His only begotten son, Jesus Christ to the world to die for our sins. Beloved this is love offering, it is a one-time offering that guarantees us to live for eternity. Apostle Paul in Romans 5:8 went further to inform us of the condition of man when this event took place; "But God demonstrates His own love toward us, in that while we were still sinners, Christ died for us." This is the express demonstration of

God's love for humanity. He declared in the book of John, "For God so loved the world that He gave His only begotten Son, that whoever believes in Him should not perish but have everlasting life. 17 For God did not send His Son into the world to condemn the world, but that the world through Him might be saved." John 3:16-17. There are so many places in the Bible where God proved His love for man.

First of all, He gave the gift of love in the person of Jesus Christ. The Scripture made it clearer as recorded in Romans 5:8, "But God demonstrates His own love toward us, in that while we were still sinners, Christ died for us." God required us to bore this in our Spirit. These revelations of God's acts points to the level of Love God has for His people. If you were to evaluate God's love on His people, then you. Will discover "Agape" kind of Love on us. Just as your wife expects you to appreciate her and wants you to tell her how much you love her, at the same token, God wants to appreciate what He did for us through obedience. He wants to bless us if we do what He said. God weighs our love for Him by how much we do what He said. Jesus said, "If you love me, keep my commandments." John 14:15.

Therefore beloved, you and I need help from His Spirit to lead us day-to-day so that we can be eligible to receive what we asked for and have the assurance of our salvation.

God's gift of salvation is freely offered to humanity, even to those who did not believe in His existence. He is always willing to forgive our sins. He still loves us but hates our sins. He declares through Apostle John, saying, "If we confess our sins, He is faithful and just to forgive us our sins and cleanse us from all unrighteousness." 1 John 1:9.

God gave us another chance to make it right by repenting from whatever sins that we have committed. He wants to see us pure before His eyes; He says no spot or wrinkles in our garment. In other words, there should be no sins of any type in our relationship with Him. We are to be Holy for Him. There is nothing we can do to quantify the love of God, which He expressed through Christ Jesus, The Bible is filled with God wooing us to respond to His love approach; that is why the Bible is the book of love. It a love letter to humanity, love of God expressed in human form.

"Greater love has no one than this: to lay down one's life for one's life for one's friends." John 15:13.

The ultimate love of God for humanity is Jesus Christ, the only son of God. God made a clear statement when He said, "Behold what manner of love the Father has bestowed on us, that we should be called children of God! Therefore the world does not know us, because it did not know Him" John 3:1.

Jesus Christ's death and resurrection are the key points of Christian faith. We believe that Jesus Christ came to the earth and was crucified on the cross, He was dead and was buried, but on the third day, God raised Him from the death. It was His sacrificial death that gave the human race the opportunity to earn eternal life in Christ Jesus. The Bible specifically said that if you confess with your mouth, the Lord Jesus Christ, and believe in your heart that God raised Him from the dead, you will be saved, Roman 10:9. The only way to deny yourselves from this special love offering is if you reject or refuse to make Jesus your only Lord and personal savior. Jesus was sacrificed for mankind. God's intent for us is to live and not die in sin. No wonder the Bible said, "You shall live and not die to declare the word of God. Paul speaking to his audience, said to live is Christ but to die is gain.

I have come across a good number of people who refused to receive Jesus Christ as their personal Lord and savior. You see, everything we do on this side of eternity is a choice, God cannot live in your heart if one is forced to make Him the Lord and savior. God loves you so much and will give you all the opportunity to repent and make Him your Lord and savior. His mercies has been towards humanity. The Bible declares:

"Through the Lord's mercies we are not consumed, because His compassions fail not. They are new every morning; great is Your faithfulness." Lamentation 3:22-23

2. God wants to bless you.

God constantly wants to bless us. His blessings know no bound. It has no limit; God is more than willing to bless us and our families. He said to Abraham, "I will make you a great nation; I will bless you and make your name great; and you shall be a blessing. I will bless those who bless you, and I will curse him who curses you; and in you all the families of the earth shall be blessed."." Genesis 12:2-3. God fulfilled all the promise He said to Abraham, and today we are all enjoying the same promise He did to Abraham. He blessed us in all things; we experience this blessing every day of our life. A songwriter reminded us to count our blessings and name them one by one, yes beloved, you can count your blessings, and you will discover that He has blessed you beyond measure.

3.   God wants to reveal His awesome personality to His people.

God intends that we know Jesus Christ, for this purpose, He becomes flesh to identify with us, and dwell among us. The word of God said, "The secret things belong to the Lord our God, but those things which are revealed belong unto us and our children forever, that we may do all the words of His law." Deuteronomy 29:29.

You see, whatever revelation we got from Him or what we learn about Him in our private encounters with Him is for our own benefits. Such revelation helps us to increase in the knowledge of Him; we trust Him for whom He said He is. Also to help us in keeping His commandments and ordinances.

God never intends for us to live separated from Him, no wonder He left heaven to earth to indwell us by His Spirit, which is why He promised never to leave us nor forsake us. He has been speaking right from the time of creation even today He still speaks and reveals to us His intentions. Whatever He said to you in His words, maybe He spoke to you through His written words or through personal encounter. All that God requires of us is belief, trust and obedience.

God revealed Pharaoh's dreams to Joseph. Joseph acted on what He said to Him. Other elites and philosophers could not tell the meaning of Pharaoh's dream, but Joseph did. As a result, Joseph was promoted to one of the highest positions in Egypt. Listen, when you obey what He said to you, He will promote you. He will increase you spiritually; He will give you good health. He will keep you safe from your adversaries and give you peace. Acting on what He said is acts of obedience. God revealed the plans of the Syrians military to destroy the Israelites and to capture Elisha. Each time the Syrians planned to attack the Israelites militarily, Elisha will act on what God said about the intentions of the Syrians plans by informing the secrets to the Israelites military commanders, Syrian's plan to invade the country of Israelites will be foiled. God was the only one that reveals the Socrates of these enemies of the Israelites. Our God is no respecter of persons, He will reveal to you any hidden plans of your enemies so that you will live to honor Him. In addition, He will protect you each time your enemies try to invade you and your family.

a.   *His blessings of mercy.*

God also blessed us with His mercy; mercy is compassion or forgiveness shown toward someone whom it is within one's power to punish or harm. The scripture says, "Through the Lord's mercies we are not consumed for His compassion fails not, they are new every morning. Great is thy faithfulness oh God." Lamentations 3:23.

God's blessing is so much on you that every single day when you go to sleep, His mercy covers all over you. When you wake up, His mercy leads you through the day. We live because of His mercy on us; when you do what He tells you to do, you will experience the abundance of His mercy. Lamentation 3:22 says, "Through the Lord's mercies we are not consumed, because His compassions fail not."

If you are going through difficulty, ask the Lord for His mercy, and grace is what we all need in this season of life. These two characteristics of God are always available for us and our loved ones.

But God's mercy stood right around us to guide us and stop the plans and purposes of the enemy against us. Jesus Christ's victory over the enemies of our lives granted us victory of a lifetime. Our victory is in His name alone. The scripture declares, "Nor is there salvation in any other, for there is no other name under heaven given among men by which we must be saved." Acts 4:12.

b. ***His Blessings of Forgiveness.***

We constantly make mistakes and trample on the commandments of God all the time. If God were to administer His judgement on us, we would all be dead one day. But, because of the great love for us, He forgives us and planned a way out of our sins, and that is the way of confession and repentance. Apostle John explained it this way:

"If we confess our sins, He is faithful and just to forgive us our sins and to cleanse us from all unrighteousness." 1 John 1:9.

What a blessing to know that your sins and mine are forgiven. As already said, this the only reason Jesus came to earth to redeem us. No one can make it to heaven if we still carry our sinful nature on him. It is a blessing to realize that God forgives our sins so that we will be free from his judgment of sins, what a glorious feeling beloved. All that Jesus Christ did at the cross made this possible, and He forgives our past present and future sins.

c. ***His Blessings of Safety.***

(Psalm 23 sums it all about His safety over you)

God is always thinking of you. He provides your safety in all things, no matter wherever you are. He makes sure that you are safe and protected. He gave you an authority in His name. The name of the Lord is a strong tower; the righteous who runs in is saved. The authority in His name guarantees you immediate victory over your enemies. Joshua commanded the sun and the moon to stand still during one the fiercest grand wars with their enemy, the moon, and the stars obeyed until God gave them victory. Peter prayed for a crippled man in the name of the Lord Jesus Christ, and the man received strength in his legs, and he immediately started walking praising God. Our afflictions, no matter how strong they are, do hear the name of Jesus Christ. They do not hear our names but the name of Jesus Christ, who got the victory.

The scripture says in the name of Jesus Christ, "That at the name of Jesus every knee should bow, of those in heaven, and of those on earth, and of those under the earth." Philippians 2:10

What a marvelous God we serve! God wants us to be safe with Him. Psalm 4:8 says:

"In peace, I will both lie down and sleep; for you alone, Lord, make me dwell in safety."

Safety is one of the primary reasons he went to the cross. He brought us into his blood covenant with Him. He sent His angels to guide us at all times. Wherever you are, he is right there with you. As a believer, you should always feel the sense of security, knowing that you are not alone; God is with you. A while ago, I experienced what I call spiritual dryness. Spiritual dryness because I felt that I was alone in my walk with God. During this period, I was not able to pray as I used to, study Bible as I used to, or fast as I used to. I was afraid of unknown things.

I complained about almost everything, both at home and at work. Trivial comments and remarks would provoke me. One day I was getting ready to do my personal Evangelism, and I felt that I was alone and that I needed someone to accompany me on this assignment. As I was contemplating over the whole thing, I heard what I believed to be "The inner witness of the Holy Spirit" saying, I have been with you at other times when you go out on evangelism, what made you think I will not be with you today? I confessed and apologized. I learnt my lesson. Other times before I go on personal Evangelism, I verbally tell the Holy Spirit that I know that He is with me, and I will say let us go, accompany me and win the lost. I am telling you that He answers. Whenever I have the assurance of His presence, I felt extraordinary bold, confident, and powerful utterance in sharing the gospel to other people. Moreover, I see more people willing to hear the gospel and gave their life over to the Lord Jesus Christ.

One day a brother said to me, "Whenever I am doing something for the kingdom of God, I feel like thousands of people are right behind me." I felt the same way sometimes when I reach out to people with the gospel. God's presence is always with us as we share the gospel. His presence surrounds us. The Bible declares:

"As the mountains surround Jerusalem, so the Lord surrounds His people from this time forth and forever." Psalms 125:2.

As already discussed above, His presence is with us at all times. He gave us assurance of His awesome presence with us, "I will never leave you nor forsake you." Hebrew 13:5.

d. *His blessings of Deliverance*

Two strong words of Christian faith that relates to deliverance are:

a. Salvation
b. Redemption.

Salvation is what Jesus Christ did for us at the cross. His sacrifice at the cross brought deliverance to humanity. Jesus Himself said "it is finished."

Redemption is buying freedom, freedom from sin. His blood blotted away our sins. We are now without sins. You know, God sees us as if we have never sinned. Therefore, beloved, the sacrificial death of Jesus Christ at the cross, brought about the total emancipation of humanity from the evil effect of sins. The acts of Jesus Christ is received by faith alone, faith in what He said in His word. It is only through faith that you and I can receive the promises of God in our life. Apostle Paul while speaking to his Roman audience said, "So then faith comes by hearing, and hearing by the word of God." Romans 10:17. You cannot develop your faith in something you don't know, or you don't hear of. For your faith to be active, you must hear the word of God and believe in Him.

Our faith is to be set on Christ's sacrifice on the cross alone. Everything about Christianity is centered on the sacrifice Jesus Christ did on the cross. Your miracles and other forms of victories are released to you as a result of the victory Jesus Christ won at the cross. His death and resurrection are like open check with your name on it. You only write your needs, and it's done. The sacrifice is one-time offer. It is not to be done again or revisited. Only our faith in Christ alone will bring the breakthroughs we need in every difficult situation that unfold daily in our lives. The word of God said, "And whatever things you ask in prayer, believing, you will receive." Matthew 21:22. Amen. The ultimate question is, who do you put your faith in? When you become sick, or you are facing other challenges of life? Who do you run to? Have you tried Jesus recently? I guarantee you that Jesus Christ is the key you need in every issue that occurs in your life. Your faith in Him releases your healing and other things you need.

CHAPTER 9

Benefits of Obedience to What God said

Responding to what God said to you releases His blessings and prompt attention to your specific needs. Evangelist Billy Graham said, "God does not call us to be successful but to be obedient." — Billy Graham.

Doing what God said is the only true way to demonstrate our love for Him. God demonstrated His love for us by His sacrificial death on the cross. There is no other way to please Him but through obedience. John 14:15 says, "If you love me keep my commandment."

Some steps to prove your love for God.

1. Receive Jesus Christ as your personal Lord and savior. Roams 10:9, John 1:12
2. Read and study the Bible daily. (God speaking to you) 2 Tim 2:15, Romans 10:17
3. Pray daily (You are speaking to God). 1 Thessalonians 5:17
4. Reach out to other people who have not come to faith in Jesus Christ and tell them about Jesus and what He did for you. 2Tim 4:5
5. Support the body of Christ by giving to your local church. 2nd Corinthians 9:6-8

6. Support the men of God as much as you can. Your support may be in financial, material, emotional, or any other kind of way they may need help.
7. Make Jesus Christ first in your life.
8. Love His people and make disciples out of them. Mark 12:30-31.

God's concerns for us:

- To save us from our sins.
- To give us eternal life.
- Rescue us from our physical and spiritual enemies.
- To fight our nettles.
- To give us good health.
- To keep us for His own glory.
- To love us always, no matter what is going on in our lives.

God delivered His message to the people through the prophets. Whenever a prophet enters a particular city, the occupants of the city began to tremble for they knew that the prophet might likely bring bad news, in 1 Kings 17:1. Prophet Elijah from Tishbe in Gilead went to King Ahab and said, I am a servant of the living Lord God of Israelites, and I swear in His name that it won't rain until I say so. There won't even be any dew on the ground. This is a message from the Lord to His people." This message is, however, not a pleasant one; the message was real and raw from God.

When the prophets receive a message from God, then they deliver the message to God's people and also inform them of the consequences of failing to obey.

Beloved, has God said something to you? When the Israelites were looking for a king to reign over them during the time of Prophet Samuel, the Prophet Samuel was a true radical prophet at the time. He brought God's message to the people of Israel. He interceded for people in prayer. The Bible said that God was displeased because of the people requesting for a king. They completely forgot the fact that God was their king who cared and led them to deliverance from bondage. However, God sent Samuel to anoint a king for them; Saul was anointed. We all know the story behind

Saul's kingship, how he disobeyed God ordinances, and the consequential fall. God also sent Prophet Samuel to Jessy's Family to anoint David, a king in place of Saul. (1ˢᵗ and 2ⁿᵈ kings)

If you give your heart to the Lord, you will automatically become one of His children. He will see you as one of his obedience servants. He will reveal your assignments to you. He will also begin to talk to reveal His awesome personality to you.

To get God's attention:

1. You must make Jesus Christ the Lord of your life.
2. Love others as God loved them.
3. Meet the spiritual and physical needs of His people.
4. Study the Bible daily and pray
5. Be available for God's service, including evangelism
6. Support Christian organizations that teach from the word of God.
7. Allow the Holy Spirit to lead you at all times.
8. Fellowship with the other believers of the same faith, The Old Testament prophets.

The people of the Old Testament depended on the prophets to reveal God's intentions. Their instructions always start this way, "Thus says the Lord God of Israel". The prophets never used their own words to deliver the message. The message received was never adulterated or enhanced. Whenever a prophet enters a city, the people begin to tremble because they think the wrath of God is about to visit them as a result of disobedience to God's instructions, or more specifically to expose their sinful acts. They also think that the prophets came to inform them of an impending disaster as a result of their sins. Prophets are God's messengers. They are ambassadors for God. You and I are ambassadors for Christ.

In other words, we carry God's message to the people. There were prophecies of His coming predicted by the prophets in the Old Testament. Isaiah's prophesied saying "Therefore the Lord Himself will give you a sign."

These two verses of the scripture in Isaiah strictly brought to focus some of the direct prophecies of the coming of Christ.

Jesus Christ is the final word of God to humanity; Jesus Christ's appearance brought to an end the law which ruled in the Old Testament, during the time of Moses. This law stipulates the animal sacrifices and shedding of its blood of the animals for the remission of sins of the people. Jesus went to the cross once and for all to shed His blood for humanity for which we are part of the community. No more animal sacrifice or its kinds. Jesus paid it all. He is our hope for living. We are alive because of what He did at the cross. The sin of Adam requires the death of the sinner. That was exactly what Christ did for humanity Apostle Paul in Romans 6:23 said it like this:

"For the wages of sin is death, but the gift of God is eternal life in Christ Jesus our Lord" Jesus Christ is also our righteousness. He took our place and died for us, so we will be free from death. We are free from eternal condemnation.

The Bible said, "For by grace you have been saved through faith, and that not of yourselves; it is the gift of God." Ephesians 2:8. Jesus Christ is a sacrificial offering to mankind. He is a love offering send to us by God almighty.

Not only did He came to die for us on the cross but also entered into blood covenant with us. Luke 22:20b.

We are covenanted through His blood. Our lives are insured in His shed blood. You and I are complete in all things partnering to heaven.

We are in a time of Grace. The grace of God ushered in the salvation of our Soul. Scripture declares that; "For God so loved the world that He gave His only begotten son that whosoever believe in Him should not perish but have everlasting life." John 3:16.

More so, the Scripture said in Ephesians 2:8-9, " For by grace you have been saved through faith, and that not of yourselves; it is the gift of God, not of works, lest anyone should boast" Simple definition of Grace says, it is unmerited favor. In other words, we are not qualified to inherit His grace as a result of sin. We all have sinned and fall short of God's glory. Romans 3:23.

The Grace of God rules the universe. Our forefathers did not enjoy this grace as a result of the fact that Jesus Christ was not in the flesh at the time. We are gracefully made and set free from the bondage of the enemy. If we understand the grace of God, then, we will stand strong, knowing that the grace of God is upon us and that eventually, we will be set free from whatever affliction we are going through. We were to stand assured of His grace. As already said, the Grace of God shadows the whole universe; we are all living and operating under the grace of God. Seen and unseen things live and move around under His Grace. Apostle Paul's letter to the Ephesians says this way, "Not of work lest any man should boast" Ephesians 2:8b. There are no human effort or strength that can satisfy our needs or the needs of our loved ones. It is only the grace of God which is in operation in the universe. Making Jesus Christ, your Lord and savior is the only way to let God know that you appreciate His grace on you.

What is your relationship with the Lord Jesus Christ? Are you living for Him or are for the world?

God's Perfections

God has been in existence before creation. He spoke the world to creation, and its contents into existence, the earth, sky moon the animals in the bush, birds of the air, in fact everything seen and unseen consists of the word of God. They all hear the word of God and respond to it. All creations portray the glory and the intelligence of God in its orientations. Everything you look at shows God's perfect craftsmanship and beautiful design He said to Himself (The trinity) that let us make man in our own image. You are created in His own image; you are a Spirit because God is a Spirit. You are a special creature. Your body was given to you so you can live and operate on earth effectively, yes, you needed it to be able to accomplish God's assignments. You are anointed to live and operate like God. The Bible declared this truth, "God is a Spirit and those who worship

Him must worship Him in Spirit and in truth" John 4:24. Yes beloved, you are a Spirit, your real self is inside of you. Your physical body is a box housing you. When your stay in this earth has ended, your real-self will return to God, and the body is deposited in the ground, and as time goes on forms part of plants food.

You are equipped and anointed to operate like God; your word should create thing. Job 22:28 declares, "You will also declare a thing, and it will be established for you; So light will shine on your ways." As an ambassador of Jesus Christ, you are to represent Him in all things; you have the power to perform miracles. To heal any manner of sickness, Jesus spoke to His disciples in line to this truth:

"Most assuredly, I say to you, he who believes in Me, the works that I do he will do also; and greater works than these he will do, because I go to My Father" John 14:11-12.

All it takes is your faith in Him, then spoke the word of God to the particular issues you want to be changed. The word spoken in faith brings results.

The universe came into existence by His word. The scripture said in the book Peter, "They consist of the word of God;" in other words, everything you see came into existence by His spoken word. Things you cannot see, but you know that they existed were also made by His words. Oh, what a glorious God we serve.

Apostle Paul speaking to the Hebrews described the word of God thus, "For the word of God is quick, and powerful, and sharper than any two-edged sword, piercing even to the dividing asunder of soul and spirit, and of the joints and marrow, and is a discerner of the thoughts and intents of the heart."

The word of God has creative power; it does what you want Him to do; it can kill and can also make alive. Deuteronomy 32:39.

The word of God, when applied in faith accomplishes all you apply it for. Your Spirit must agree with the Spirit of God to get results; you must be born again! Only those born again Christians can claim the gift of eternal life. Do you have faith in the risen Christ?

CHAPTER 10

God's Final Words: His Son

"God, who at various times and in various ways spoke in time past to the fathers by the prophets, has in these last days spoken to us by His Son, whom He has appointed heir of all things, through whom also He made the worlds." Hebrews 1:1-2. Jesus is the complete revelation of God's presence to humanity.

As already discussed, God spoke through the seers, dreams, and other ways, including the prophets. All these are a type of Jesus Christ in the context, in the Old Testament. The Scripture made it clear that God finally spoke to Man (Humanity) through His only son Jesus Christ. We should not be expecting any other ways to hear from God, but through His only begotten son Jesus Christ. Therefore, beloved, it is important to hear what God is saying through His son Jesus Christ. God said, "Be still and know that I am God." What God was saying to the people of the Old Testament is understandably stated in the New Testament. First, about the coming of His son Jesus Christ, death, and resurrection. These three Biblical theologies are the pillars of Christianity. Apostle Paul declared, "For I determined not to know anything among you except Jesus Christ and Him crucified." 1 Corinthians 2:2.

In these last days...

God has always wanted His people to live for Him alone. He wanted absolute obedience from us. Sins have continued to be the impediment to total worship and obedience. As already mentioned, God spoke to His people in the Old Testament through various ways to flee from idol worship and other forms of sins. The animal sacrifices they offered to appease to God could not wipe away their sins permanently. Hebrews 10:4 says, "For it is not possible that the blood of bulls and goats could take away sins."

Man's greatest enemy.

Man's problem is sin. God has great love for sinners. He, however, hates sins in them. As a result of His love for us, He decided to deal with the issue of sins once and for all. The Scripture says that the punishment for sin is death.

Eternal life in hell awaits for sinners. Therefore to avert God's judgement on sinners, He sent His only begotten son to die for the sins of the whole world for which you and I are part of it. Jesus Christ was crucified on the Cross. Matthew 27:32-56: John 19:24. Romans 5:8 further says, "But God demonstrates His own love toward us, in that while we were still sinners, Christ died for us." Yes, he died on the Cross and was buried, but on the third day, he rose from the dead. He is alive today.

This passage also confirms that we are all living in the last days. There are other passages of the Bible that speaks about last days. 2 Timothy 3: 1, "But know this, that in the last days perilous times will come".......2 Peter 3:3-4, Luke 21:25-26, Matthew 24:42-44, Daniel 12:4

All these passages and many others talk about the last days and events that have occurred, which points to the fact that we are living in the last days. All the Bible prophecies concerning the last days have been fulfilled. Jesus Christ is coming very soon, are you ready?

Waiting for the last days.

In anticipation of the end of the age and the second coming of Christ, the question now is, what are you going to do as you wait for the event of the last days to unfold? This obvious question leads us to the title of this book, "What God said to you." Honest answer to this question gives you an insight of your responsibility during this perilous times of living, and also how to watch for the sound of the trumpet. But in general, Apostle Peter admonishes us to live peacefully and to live without spots or wrinkles in our lives, meaning living for Jesus Christ as your only Lord and savior. God's anger for sin is erased permanently in your life when you accept the free gift of salvation in Jesus Christ as your personal savior. "Therefore, beloved, looking forward to these things, be diligent to be found by Him in peace, without spot and blameless." 2 Peter 3:14.

As we participate in the kingdom-building, we are also to watch and pray.

- Do the work of an evangelist.
- Preach in season and out of season (2Tim. 4:2)
- Pray without season. 1 Thessalonians 5:17
- Walk with Christ daily as you receive Him. Do not lack in the knowledge of Him.
- Let Him be your true Lord and savior.
- "As you therefore have received Christ Jesus the Lord, so walk in Him, rooted and built up in Him and established in the faith, as you have been taught, abounding in it with thanksgiving." Col.2:6-7
- "Set your mind on things above, not on things on the earth." Colossians 3:2

Have a quiet time to meet with the Lord when you rise and before you go to bed. These do not interfere with you praying your way within the day. Before I started writing on this topic, I taught my children how to live for the Lord alone. They always pray early in the morning before they leave for school and pray again before they go to sleep. I tried to inculcate in them the habit of prying at all times, not only when challenges come but also when there are no challenges. A prayerful Christian is a powerful Christian. A prayer-less is a powerless Christian.

Hate what is evil. Hold unto what is good. Romans 12:9. Choose to hate what God hates and love what God loves. You are a child of God, nothing less. Do not allow yourself to fall into devils lies; he will come to tell you that you are not, he will try to remind you of some lies and other forms of sins you committed in the past. Do not believe Him for the Bible says that your sins have been bolted out by the powerful blood of Jesus Christ. You are a new creature, sinless and pure soul. If you sinned, listen to the word of God in 1ˢᵗ John 1:9, "If we confess our sins, He is faithful and just to forgive us our sins and to cleanse us from all unrighteousness." You are not to sin willfully for the Bible says that sins committed in ignorance are forgiven, the blood of Jesus Christ cleanses you. We must be careful not to sin willfully. The Bible made this clearer in Acts 17:30, "Truly, these times of ignorance God overlooked, but now commands all men everywhere to repent."

Who is Jesus Christ to you?

Jesus Christ is the central figure of Christian beliefs. Without Jesus Christ, in the picture, there will be nothing like Christianity. No one can do what He did for humanity. He lived to die for you and me and rose again for our justification.

The theology of justification is simply declaring or making righteous in the sight of God. In other words, you and I are free from the bondage of sins of the past, present, and future. The conclusion of the matter in the New Testament is the resurrection of Jesus Christ. When Jesus Christ was on the cross He made a very clear statement which further assured us of our total emancipation from the wages of sin:

After this Jesus knowing that all things were now accomplished, that scripture might be fulfilled, said, "I Thirst." Now a vessel full of sour wine was sitting there; and they filled a sponge with sour wine, put it on hyssop, and put it to His mouth. So when Jesus had received the sour wine, he said, "IT IS FINISHED," and bowing His head he gave up his Spirit. John 19:28-30. Nobody has the power to accomplish what Jesus Christ did for humanity. When Jesus said "It is finished," he was invariably assuring the world that all the prophecies about his coming, which were prophesied from Genesis to the book of Malachi, are fulfilled. No other sacrifice could certify the requirement needed to set man free, but the one Jesus did at the cross. No more animal sacrifices, we now have direct access with God the father.

God's Spirit.

As a result of His love for us, he indwells us by His Spirit to help us live the kind of life He desired for all of us. "Or do you not know that your body is the temple of the Holy Spirit who is in you, whom you have from God, and you are not your own?" 1 Corinthians 6:19.

God, through prophet Ezekiel, went further in this assurance of His indwelling of the Holy Spirit said, "I will put My Spirit within you and cause you to walk in My statutes, and you will keep My judgments and do them." Ezekiel 36:27. Listen beloved, one of the secondary reasons Jesus Christ came was to indwell us so he can reach out to the humanity through us so that they too will have eternal life. Jesus wants to save everyone for the love of God is for every person. When you receive Jesus Christ by faith into your life as Lord and savior, he indwells you, all ready to reveal His awesome personality to you. So whenever you stand preaching or sharing the word of to the unbelievers, he is right there with you speaking to the one you are ministering through His word which you are speaking.

When Jesus was still with His disciples in the flesh, he revealed to them his awesome personality and his purpose of coming to the earth. He asked them some specific and important questions which I believe is still very relevant to us today.

1. "Who do men said that I am? Matthew 16:13. And they answered Him; some say that thou art John the Baptist. Some Elias; and

others Jeremiahs, or one of the prophets. Matthew 16:14 He said unto them.

2. But who do you say that I am? Matthew 16:15.

Simon Peter answered and said, "You are the Christ, the Son of the living God." Matthew 16:16. Jesus answered and said unto him, "Blessed are you, Simon Bar-Jonah, for flesh and blood has not revealed this to you, but My Father who is in heaven." 16:17. The proceeding verse strategized one of the purposes of our availability and responsibility to our Lord Jesus Christ.

God's desire for us is not only for us to make Him our Lord and savior but also to respond to His offer of love. That is why the ministers especially leaders in our congregations should emphasize to a great extent the importance of daily Bible study. We must also make it a point of duty to emphasize or teach on the Gift of eternal life. You need the Holy Spirit to be able to perceive and understand what God is saying in His word. Invite the Holy Spirit each time you are about to study the Bible. The Scripture said, "Faith comes by hearing and hearing by the word of God." Romans 10:17.

Beloved of God, Faith is the key to intimacy with God. Therefore, it becomes necessary for you and me to work on our faith in Him. First is the evidence of things hoped for; it is the appearance of things not seen. It is the spiritual condition of the heart, which can increase and decrease depending on us. If you believe that there is God, then apply your faith in Him, and He will work for you. Jesus Christ wants his disciple to know who He is and to develop their faith in Him, that is why He asked them; "who do you say I am."

Keys to knowing who Jesus is?

1. Invite Him to be your personal Lord and savior.
2. Pray every day(pray without ceasing also)
3. Study your Bible daily to know Him better. When you read the Bible (includes studying it) God talks to you.

4. Apply what He said to you from the Bible to your daily living code. You can practice living righteously for Him.

5. Attend a Bible-believing church. Do not be a sit down Christian; rather, participate in whatever you are assigned to do, do it without complaining. There is a reward for everything you do faithfully for Christ, your reward starts right here on the earth and continues when you go home to the Lord in heaven.

6. Share your faith regularly with other people who have not come to Christ. Start with your family, then your friends and others outside your family circle. Let the Holy Spirit lead while you follow. You will never regret His leadership. He speaks through you to the person you are about to share the word of God with. Your availability is of utmost importance to Him.

Apostle Peter had first-hand information of whom Jesus Christ is. He trusted Jesus and followed Him faithfully, God saw his innocence and willing desire to follow his master Jesus, and then He revealed Jesus Christ to him. Peter, in answer to the question Jesus posed to them, said "Thou art Christ the son of the living God," Jesus confirmed that Peter answered correctly. As already mentioned above, knowing who Jesus is the first step to knowing God. Therefore knowing Him:

1. Changes our perception of who God is, His trio, and His omnipotent nature.

2. Changes our approach to Him. We come to Him with thanksgiving and appreciation.

3. Help us relate to other people with the love of Jesus Christ in our hearts.

4. We now focus on His love and eternity in Him after our stay on this side of eternity has ended.

5. We now began to love what He loves and hate what He hates.

6. Our love for Him leads us to study the Bible more, more fellowships with other believers, and engage in kingdom-building by reaching out to the community.

How to recognize God's voice?

Truthfully, in the cause of our everyday living, there are various kinds of voices trying to capture our attention. These voices set our emotions for decision, based on certain principles, on matter we are about to undertake. Have you ever made a decision on some issues, and after some periods of time, you began to doubt if you have made a right decision, especially if it is not working out the way you had planned. I personally encountered several of such rash decisions. This kind of decision without consulting God always end up on a comment that says had I known I wouldn't have been too quick to take this decision. Often, we turn around to blame or to feel dejected thinking that God had forgotten us, or a feeling of being punished for certain sin. Beloved, it is not so; however, God wants us to commit our concerns to Him. Peter speaking to his audience said, "Casting all your care upon Him, for He cares for you" 1 Peter 5:7.

God loves us so much to the level that He is willing to guide us all the way in making decision no matter how small or insignificant such decisions are. For us to make decisions based on what He said to us requires us to recognize His voice. The first principle that I will like to discuss is:

Learn to recognize His voice.

One simple truth we all should know about God is that He speaks uniquely to us daily. He talks and walks with us daily. He desires fellowship with you and I, have you ever prayed to the extent that you do not want to stop, your whole being is consumed in that secret moment with Him to the extent that you don't even know that someone is around. Have you ever recognize His voice as you study the Scripture? Have you ever heard in your spirit as God speaks to you? God specifically speaks to us through His Spirit. He speaks to us on the issues that are of our concern. Talking to us is one of the reasons He indwells by His Spirit. As already mentioned, when God speaks, He expects us to listen and follow through and do what He said. Recognizing God's voice starts with your personal relationship with His son Jesus Christ.

If however you do not experience the level of the relationship after you believe that you have made Him your Lord and savior, then something is wrong, maybe unconfessed sins or you had mental accented confession, or your believe is not from your heart.

Sin is our problem.

Sin is the only weapon that can stand between God and us. Isaiah 59:1-2. But, because God loves us so much that He provided a way out of our sins so that we can hear His voice clearly. The Bible said in 1 John 1:9:

"If we confess our sins, He is faithful and just to forgive us and to cleanse us from all unrighteousness."

So beloved, if you pray and not feel the presence of God, stop, assess your conducts for the day to see if there is any sin you encountered. No matter how insignificant it may seem, maybe you need to forgive someone, then, confess it before the Lord and move on with your life and continue to do what He asked you to do. Always remember that God is not a man He does not reason the way we do. He loves you and has paid for that particular sin on the Cross. Be honest with Him. He is more than willing to forgive you if you are honest in your ways with Him.

Ultimately the question we should ask ourselves is, how do we recognize the voice of God from all the crowded voices that filter into our minds daily, which of them can we label as God's voice. When we recognize His voice, we can perceive clearly what He is saying and act on it.

How to recognize God's Voice.

The key point in recognizing the voice of God starts with:

- Your relationship with His son Jesus Christ.
- Recognize His Holy Spirit and allow Him to lead your life.

- Obey God's commandments. (This includes reaching to His people with His love.)

If you recognize these 3 principles written above, God will trust you. He will see you as an honest son. His Spirit will bring clarity to the voice of God, and you will be able to differentiate the voice of God from other voices out there.

a.   Increase of our Faith in Him:

The Bible declares that Faith comes by hearing the word of God, Romans 10:17. You see, Faith is the leading factor to receiving the promises of God, which He said we can have. Essentially it is important to build up your faith by believing and acting on His promises.

Faith is alive and living. Without faith, it is impossible to please God. Yes, faith is a very sure avenue to be a friend of God.

b.   Build up confidence and boldness to trust Him.

From the word of God, you can also build your confidence and boldness. Boldness is a result or fruit of your faith in Him. The scripture says that God indwells you by His Spirit. One of the reasons He indwells you is to give you boldness and confidence so that we can serve Him without fear or trembling. He empowers you and me with extraordinary gifts of anointing for effective witness of His salvation message to the world. When God calls you, He equips you with all you need to be an effective servant. 2 Corinthians 3:11-12 says, "For if what is passing away was glorious, what remains is much more glorious. Therefore, since we have such hope, we use great boldness of speech" As already said, faith is the leading factor to boldness and confidant in Him.

c.   Assurance.

He gives us the assurance that what we are petitioning for we have it. Assurance is a product of our faith in the Lord. First, we hear the word, faith shows up, then boldness and confidence shows up, then, assurance.

Assurance is a positive declaration intended to give confidence. Sometimes when I minister salvation message to someone, I usually ask those who claim that they have already received Jesus as Lord and savior. A question like this, "Do you have assurance of your salvation? Do you confident in your declaration of your faith in Christ Jesus?

As a Christian you must have the assurance of the fact that Christ lives in you, and that you will be in heaven with the Lord if you were to die. You must have the undiluted assurance of faith that Jesus Christ is what "He said He is" and the assurance of the fact that Jesus is alive. Satan is afraid of a Christian who has assurance of their belief because he (devil) knows that you know what you are talking about when you said that you are Christ follower. Those who do not have assurance of their salvation deny the existence of our lord and savior. They are unsure of what they believe.

As already discussed above, faith in Jesus Christ is the foundation of well-balanced Christianity. Yes, when God speaks, it is different from any other voice which you hear on a daily basis. Studying the word of God daily and doing what it says catapult our faith to a higher spiritual cadre in serving the Lord.

$$\frac{\text{Believe+}}{\text{Hearing + Determination}} = \text{Take Action}$$

^	^	^
You heard	You determine to take action	Do what you heard.

1. Submission

We are to submit to the Lordship of Jesus Christ by inviting Him into our lives as personal Lord and savior. The Scripture says that when we do this, He comes in and indwells us by His Spirit. 2 Corinthians 12:10. It is only through personal relationship that we can recognize His voice and increase our faith in him.

2. Study the Bible daily:

God speaks to us through His inspired word in the Bible. Bible said, "All Scripture is given by inspiration of God, and is profitable for doctrine, for reproof, for correction, for [a]instruction in righteousness, 17 that the man of God may be complete, thoroughly equipped for every good work." 2 Timothy 3:16-17.

3. Obey

Obey every commandment of the Lord Jesus Christ even if it does not make sense to you. God qualifies us as His children if we obey His commands. The Scripture even made it clearer in John 14:15; "If you love me, keep my commandments." The ultimate purpose of God's commandment for us is for our blessings. He wants to bless you; the blessings come as you keep His commandments. Keeping God's commandment is absolute obedience. It is respect to the almighty God. You are, in actuality giving total surrender to His will. So beloved of God, you will be a qualified child of God with no wrinkles or spot in your relationship with Him.

4. Pray at all times.

Be honest in your prayer; tell God every detail of your life, ask Him questions. Your faith in Him brings you closely connected to Him. He loves you very much. He listens and cares for every one of us when we call on Him God loves every one of us equally. He call on us continually to obey His commandments so we can enjoy all that He has blessed us with. The Scripture declares, "For there is no partiality with God. For as many as have sinned without law will also perish without law, and as many as have sinned in the law will be judged by the law" Romans 2:11-12.

5. Confess and repent from your sins.

If you fall into any type of sin, no matter what the sin may be, immediately repent and confess it to God. Do not visit such an act of sin again, but look unto God. Ask the Holy Spirit who indwells you to give you strength to overcome all manner of sins. All of the God's 'generals' in the Bible have fallen into one or the other type of sin. But one beautiful thing they did was to realize that they have fallen into sin, the next beautiful thing they did was to confess such sin to God, repent and ask God to cleanse you with His blood. The scripture made it clearer to us:

"But if we walk in the light, as He is in the light, we have fellowship one with another, and the blood of Jesus Christ, His son cleanse us from all sin."1 John 1:7. Believing God's word to concerning you, you forgive yourself as soon as you confess such sin to God. According 1 John 1:9 which say:

"If we confess our sins, He is faithful and just to forgive us our sins and to cleanse us from all unrighteousness." then focus on doing what God said to you. Immediately you act on what He said to you, no matter what it is, the result of what you acted on is seen. Can I ask you a question? What did God said to you?

As already discussed above, every word of God, as written in the Bible, is a direct instruction to humanity and how to live for Him in holiness so as to earn eternity with Him. We are to live to His direction, and it precepts that pleases Him. The word of God is a love story of God's love for mankind. As you and I are alive and breathing, so is the word of God. Yes, He is; He does all your heart desired Him to do if you approach Him with unadulterated faith. The word is Jesus Christ in print, and if you obey His word, He will love you and count you among the elects. The book of John made it clearer, "In the beginning was the word and the word was with God and the word was God." John 1:1

Friends, it then becomes absolutely important for a child of God to be consistent in studying the word in such a manner, and with a renewed faith in Him.

You are complete in Him.

"For in Him dwells all the fullness of the Godhead bodily; and you are complete in Him, who is the head of all principality and power." Colossians 2:9-10. To be complete means to be furnished with all things necessary for our salvation.

The salvation of our Soul was the ultimate reason Jesus Christ came to the world. It is available to everyone that wants it. Salvation of our soul is the central message of the church, for God does not want any of us to perish, but to have life and to have it more abundantly. Apostle Paul explained it further, "For He made Him who knew no sin to be sin for us, that we might become the righteousness of God in Him." 2 Corinthians 5:21.

Beloved, what else can we ask for. You and I, and the rest of humanity, have been delivered by the sacrifice Jesus did through the most gruesome death he experienced on the cross. We were set free from what could've been a life of doom for humanity. He did this because of the love He had for us. The Scripture said, "Behold what manner of love the Father has bestowed on us, that we should be called children of God! Therefore the world does not know us, because it did not know Him." 1 John3:1

Inner witness of the Holy Spirit.

The presence of God's Holy Spirit indwelling you does a good job of revealing the mind of God. He reveals who He is and God's intentions for your life. When God said a thing to you, His Spirit receives the instruction in you and illuminates your heart with His joy. This joy causes you to praise Him, as you and I know that His blessings manifest. You know, blessings of God come to you when you willingly obey Him in His word. Note, there is a blessing attached to every time you obey the word of God. We should, therefore, strive hard to obey whatever God said to us with zeal and love.

The indwelling of the Holy Spirit also helps you to achieve whatever God said to you. To buttress this information in a clearer form goes this way:

The indwelling Holy Spirit helps you carry out the assignment in a manner that is pleasing and acceptable to the almighty God. You should not carry out the assignments according to the worldly standard.

Sometimes, in our natural minds, we think of what God said as meaningless instructions, and so, it becomes a reason for us not to act on what He said. Listen, every word of God is alive and living, it transforms an individual and gives such individual a purpose for living. The Holy Spirit illuminates our hearts with what He said, in addition, He enables us to act on such instructions. God sees the things our eyes cannot see, He knows man's ways. Another way in which we can get the revelation of God is by making Him our personal Lord and savior. More so, doing what He said to us in His word. A believer of Jesus Christ is expected to live a life of obedience, doing all He said in His word. We must continually strive to keep His commandments to become loved child of God. Obedience is the key to been called a man of God. With life of obedience, you are positioned to enjoy the blessings of God. He trusts you and sees you as His friend.

Living a life of appreciation.

The word appreciation means an expression of admission, approval, or gratitude to someone who had done a favor to you. We all want some to appreciate for any kind of favor we did.

Sometimes ago, someone told me that she wants people to show appreciation whenever she does a good deed to them. You want someone to say, 'Hey! I really appreciate your favor you showed me the other day, thanks a lot'.

Similarly, God desired us to show appreciation to Him for what He did for us on the cross. He suffered because of my sins, yours, and the whole world. He was crucified on the wooden cross for an offense He did not commit. No man living or dead has ever done what He did for humanity. He saved us and offered us life in eternity in Him. Eternity means infinite, and it talks of endless life which means we will not die anymore. We will live forever in Him. Paul speaking to his audience said:

"We are confident, yes, well pleased rather to be absent from the body and to be present with the Lord" 2 Corinthians 5:8. We will all spend eternity with Him in heaven. The scripture declares that He has gone to prepare a place for you and me.

"Let not your heart be troubled; you believe in God, believe also in Me. In My Father's house are many mansions; if it were not so, I would have told you. I go to prepare a place for you. And if I go and prepare a place for you, I will come again and receive you to Myself; that where I am, there you may be also." John 14:1-3. These words spoken by Jesus Christ, Himself, are comforting words for everyone. We hold unto His words as we go through the life journey. His word is our assurance as we walk through the narrow and thorny way, whose end of it is life. So beloved, how do we live life of appreciation.

Ten beautiful ways to show appreciation to God

1. Receive Jesus Christ as Lord and savior. It is respect and responsible act for you to strive to know who God is. God smiles on you when you become a God chaser. Jesus is the Image of the invisible God. The firstborn of all creations. Colossians 1:15. To know God is to know Jesus. Jesus revealed to His disciples, "I am the way, the truth, and the life. No one comes to the Father except through Me." John 14:6. Receiving Jesus as your personal Lord and savior is one of the greatest commandments from God. Knowing all these truths and bearing them in your Spirit positions you to appreciate God even more.
2. Always pray a prayer of thanksgiving, lifting up your hands in adoration.
3. Always appreciate God in your life for what He is doing. Practice at all times. Praying is one of Jesus Christ's constant practice. Prayer is two-way communication between God and you.
4. Obey every commandment as written in His book and thank Him for His enablement.

5. Give thanks to Him for His numerous benefits to us. Appreciate His Grace He supplied to carry us daily in the mist challenges we experience daily.
6. Serve others with love, share what you have, and meet their needs. Do not expect rewards.
7. Visit the sick and the prisoners
8. Share the good news of salvation.
9. Participate in kingdom-building programs such as bringing people to Christ through evangelism. Help in the local church and serve the Lord with all your love and might.
10. Appreciate God for who He is. As He continues to bless you, do not brush it aside. Let Him know that you appreciate His presence and His blessings in your life and your loved ones. Share your testimony whenever you have an opportunity.

God is honored when we give Him thanks

When Jesus was traveling to Jerusalem, the Scripture said, "Now it happened as He went to Jerusalem that He passed through the midst of Samaria and Galilee. Then as He entered a certain village, there met Him ten men who were lepers, who stood afar off. And they lifted up their voices and said, "Jesus, Master, have mercy on us!" So when He saw them, He said to them, "Go, show yourselves to the priests." And so it was that as they went, they were cleansed. And one of them, when he saw that he was healed, returned, and with a loud voice glorified God, and fell down on his face at His feet, giving Him thanks. And he was a Samaritan. So Jesus answered and said, "Were there not ten cleansed? But where are the nine? Were there not any found who returned to give glory to God except this foreigner?" And He said to him, "Arise, go your way. Your faith has made you well."." Luke 17:19

It gladdens the heart of God when we show appreciation to Him for His goodness to us; He also wants us to share with others what he did for us, by this they will know that there is God who loves them unconditionally. Do you share with others what good the Lord had done for you?

In fact, sharing the testimony of what God has done for you is one of the powerful evangelical tools for saving souls for eternity in heaven. Your testimony of His everyday blessings also serves as a tool to build confidence in God for the hearers.

Total sum of God's intentions for Man.

The Salvation of our soul is the total sum of God's purpose for mankind. Everything about God is in His word. The word of God is God and God is His word, John 1:1. Additionally, whatever God said to you has the life of God in it, if you obey, it gives you life and nourishes your soul. God cannot tell you to do something that will not benefit you. We are always on a receiving side. He gave us victory over all things. Our responsibility as believers must be to discover who God is. This can be possible if we have made Him our personal Lord and savior, fellowship with other faithful believers, study the bible, and pray at all times. Our pastors and those who are called are to emphasize the need for Bible study and live daily on what it says. The reason being for the individual to develop an intimate personal relationship with Him.

The old and the New Testament.

The Word of God covers all the Old Testament, which has a total of 39 books and the New Testament 27 books. All these reveal to us the mind and the intentions of God for humanity. It is a book of love, it talks of the love of God for humanity. It also talks of life in eternity.

Bible is intelligently written and gives us the firsthand information of who God is. His rescue plan intended to rescue man from sin and give eternal life with Him. It starts with:

1. His love for the world. John 3:16

"For God so loved the world that He gave His only begotten Son, that whoever believes in Him should not perish, but have everlasting life. For

God sent not His son into the world to condemn the world; but that the world through Him might be saved" John 3:16-17.

    2.   His death on the Cross.

His death on the Cross blots out the handwriting of ordinances that was against us, which was contrary to us and took it out of the way, nailing it to the His cross; And having spoiled principalities and powers, he made a show of them openly triumphing over them in it. Colossians 2:14-15. Beloved every accusation of the enemy against you is nullified, you are as clean as you have never sinned before. Satan has nothing to tag on you and me. We are cleansed from all our sins, which we inherited from Adam and Eve. We are complete in Christ, yes we are. (Colossians 2:10.) You and I need no other sacrifices; the deal is done and we are free forever. As a Christian who knew his position in Christ, we ought to be excited, knowing that we are free for eternity.

Buried in the grave with sins of all people on Him, the grave was a moment of decision between good and evil. Satan, the father of evil, thought that his desire had been accomplished, until the moment of decision when suddenly Jesus Christ rose from the dead after 3 days rendering the grave empty. Colossians 2:25.

The grave cannot hold Him. The book of Acts declares "Whom God raised up, having loosed the pains of death, because it was not possible that He should be held by it." Acts 2:24.

Before the creation of the world, God had us in mind, and the reason for our salvation came into play after Adam and his wife Eve, sinned by disobeying God's commandments. The consequence of expulsion from the gardens of Eden was a result of their action. Genesis 3:24.

In other words, they were driven out of the presence of God; they were separated from God's fellowship with them. The Bible declares that God hates sins but loves sinners. It is only our sins that can separate us from His attention and His presence. The Bible said in Isaiah 59:2:

"But your iniquities have separated you from your God; and your sins have hidden His face from you, so that He will not hear."

God loves us so much and wants to fellowship with us at all times, for Adam and Eve, the Bible said that God comes to fellowship with them in the cool of the day, I suppose, in the evening of the day.

When Adam sinned, they lost that fellowship. It is the same thing with us; whenever we sin against God, we lose His ultimate presence, but His love is still available. As a result of His love for us when Adam fell, God put in place a total new concept to bring us back to Him, and that is the "plan of salvation."

The love of God for us is immeasurable; it can never be compared with any other love we have involved with before. He does not want anything to hinder Him from loving us. 1 John 3:1 says, "Behold what manner of love the Father has bestowed on us, that we should be called children of God! Therefore the world does not know us, because it did not know Him."

In the same manner, Paul speaking to his audience said:

"Who shall separate us from the love of Christ? Shall tribulation, or distress, or persecution, or famine, or nakedness, or peril, or sword?" Romans 8:35.

My question to you remains the same; have you perceived the love of God in your life? Do you actually think of God's love for you? Have you paused sometimes and count His blessings on you and your loved ones? If you don't see His ultimate presence, then think about life He gave to you day after day. He allowed you to live, some of your age mates have passed, but you are still alive. His Grace and mercy leads you as He wakes you up every day. In addition, God said to you, "God into this day and be happy in it."

The benefits of acting on what God said to you.

Acting on what God said to you is an act of obedience. He weighs your love for Him through obedience.

As you require your son or daughter to obey your instructions; the God also requires you and I to obey His instructions. God is more serious when it comes to the concept of obedience. Jesus Christ is a symbol of obedience to God. His obedience resulted to our beautiful future and hope of eternal life. God's hidden treasures for His people is imbedded in obedience to what He said. The test of our obedience to God started right from the Garden of Eden with Adam and Eve. The Lord commanded the man saying:

"And the Lord God commanded the man, saying, "Of every tree of the garden you may freely eat; 17 but of the tree of the knowledge of good and evil you shall not eat, for in the day that you eat of it you[a] shall surely die."" Genesis 2:16-17

It was man's disobedience that threw the world into confusion and difficulties that all of us are experiencing today. The book of Deuteronomy sums the benefits of obedience this way; Deuteronomy 11:26-28.

Behold, I set before you today a blessing and a curse:

- "The blessing, if you obey the commandments of the Lord your God which I command you today.
- And the curse, if you do not obey the commandments of the Lord your God, but turn aside from the way which I command you today, to go after other gods which you have not known."

Obedience to what God said to you is a beautiful pathway into advancing to knowledge and an intimate relationship with Jesus Christ. It is the will of God for you to have intimate relationship with Him. You are the reason for His coming to the earth, so He cannot let you go until His purpose is fulfilled in your life.

The whole duty of man.

"Let us hear the conclusion of the whole matter, "Fear God and keep His commandments" Ecclesiastes 12:13

Online Dictionary definition of fear means an unpleasant emotion caused by the belief that someone or something dangerous is likely to cause pain or a threat.

Theologically, fear means willingly express Holy awe or reverence of God and His laws which springs from a just view and real love of the divine character, leading the subjects of it to hate and shun everything that can offend such a holy being and incline them to aim at perfect obedience.

As already mentioned in our discussion, God's highest expectation of a man is to receive the love offering He presented to mankind in the person of Jesus Christ and to keep His commandments as well. A true Christian practices to obey God in every ramification of life. Also a true Christian shuns everything or anything that might interfere with his relationship with the creator. You see, lack of trust, ego, and selfishness seems to be the major problem defocusing us from total submission and trust to God. I had to confess my sins of lack of trust in God when my wife was ill. My first reaction was to look for a Doctor. Do not misunderstand me at this; I will like to seek the attention of a doctor if there is a need for it, but the point I want to make is that doctor should not be our first person to consult; God is. He promised us everything thing we need, including healing us from any kind of sickness or disease. Immediately, I confessed to God and went ahead to pray and committed the sickness to God and asked for healing. There is nothing wrong in seeing your doctor, but first we should present our afflictions to God. We are so ignorant that we sidetrack God in almost everything until we get into trouble, then we turn around and ask Him. The scripture said commit your ways into the hands of God and He will see you through.

The truth is that our calling is a calling of obedience. If we obey God, everything about us falls into place. Listen to the word of God through Brother Matthew:

"But seek first the kingdom of God and His righteousness, and all these things shall be added to you." Matthew 6:33

All these things that shall be added to your blessings:

- Good health
- Good family
- Good job
- Good wife
- Good husband
- Good children.

In fact, all that you desire or need will be taken care of-- all the promises of the Bible according to Deuteronomy will be yours.

God's plan of salvation

God originally spoke to mankind through the prophets, seers, dreams, and other ways of His choice. Correspondingly they responded to what God said to them. As a result of their obedience to God's voice, their names became one of the limelight's in the Bible, from Genesis to Revelation. When they disobeyed God and realized what they did, they immediately humble themselves and seek His repentance and confession. Beloved, this is what God expected from His children. They also forgive themselves. The Scripture declares, "If we confess our sins, He is faithful and just to forgive us our sins and to cleanse us from all unrighteousness." 1 John 1:9

These servants of God were seen as God's general or men of God as a result of their willingness to obey God no matter what it takes. Also, they have seen God's faithfulness in meeting the needs of His people.

It is wise for someone who considers himself a Christian to hear what God said and follow through to fulfilling the instructions given. As already discussed above, there is a blessing attached to every point of obedience to God's instructions. God basically commanded us to obey and live.

God finally spoke to all generations in these last days by His son Jesus Christ, whom He appointed all things and through whom also He made the worlds. Hebrews 1:2. You are included in the generation spoken off. The Bible expressly declares, "Looking unto Jesus, the author and finisher of our faith, who for the joy that was set before Him endured the cross, despising the shame, and has sat down at the right hand of the throne of God." Hebrews 12:2a. Jesus Christ fulfilled God's desire for mankind by way of the Cross. We are to without iota of doubt accept this sacrifice in our hearts.

The critical point of our acceptance is to invite Jesus in our heart to be our Lord and savior. When this confession is made in faith, His Holy Spirit, which indwells us now continually directs our attention to Him as we study His word, and enable us to grow in knowledge and faith in Him.

Obviously, we are not expecting another sacrifice. The crucifixion of Jesus Christ, the only son of God on the Cross, is one-time sacrifice in this generation or future generations. We are totally set free forever, no more bondage, no more chain. Alleluia.

Your responsibility

Have you ever asked yourself this important question; "what are my responsibilities to God"? What does God expect me to be doing at this time of my life?

As soon as you ponder on these questions, I believe that the Holy Spirit will fill your mind with the answer to these obvious questions. God has a purpose for you. It is regrettable that a lot of people, especially believers in the Lord have not found their God-given purpose in life. God can never hide your purpose for you; you are the one who have not asked for it. The Bible reminds us that if you seek Him, you will be found by Him (1 Chronicles 28:9c).

God is speaking to you; whether through the inner witness of the Holy Spirit or word of knowledge or through the prophet or through the dreams all has Biblical backups. God cannot tell you to do something outside His mind. You can dig out what God wants you to do from the Bible. God cannot deny Himself or His word. As already mentioned, His Holy Spirit indwells you to reveal His purpose for your life.

Summary of God's word to the church.

"Let us hear the conclusion of the whole matter:

Fear God and keep His commandments, for this is man's all." Ecclesiastes 12:13.

The season we are in is a season of obedience. It is a season to act on what God said. We have no time to waste but to begin immediately to act on what He said in His Bible.

The proceeding verse in Ecclesiastes said, "For God will bring every work into judgment, including every secret thing, whether good or evil." Ecclesiastes 12:14.

The word fear in this context refers to the reverend, a deep reference for God. Loving Him and loving His people as well as maintaining an unadulterated relationship with Him. God wants His children to a total commitment to obedience. Again Proverbs 1:7 says,

"The fear of the Lord is the beginning of knowledge, but fools despise wisdom and instruction." This chapter and verse give us some added antithetical parallelism to our discussion on Life and the Foolish life. A wise person fears and references the Lord, but a foolish person despises the word of God.

The Bible said emphatically said that everything we did must be judged, both things we did in the open and things we did in a hidden manner, all must pass through the fire of God to check our motives. Our motive in the service of the Lord must have its foundation of our Love for God. It must be because we love Him any other motive for our service will attract the wrath of God. Beloved it is then that rewards will be distributed according to what we did during our life spent on earth.

How to retain what God said to you.

1. Study: It is to devote time and attention to acquire knowledge.

Study the Bible daily, and whatever God said to you in the chapter or passage, go through it within the day. Meditate on it, think about it memorize it. Put it into practice. Before you go into the next study, review what God said in the previous chapters you studied. Look at it again and meditate on it before you start another chapter.

2. Listening: It is an active emotional response to action. We can listen to what pleases us and may decide not to pay attention to the action.

Listening is an important element in our everyday living if you don't listen, you will not be able to hear what someone is saying to you. God requires us to always listen to what is being said to us on a daily basis. Without active listening, we may not correctly carry out the instructions that please Him. Proverb 19:20 says, "Listen to counsel and receive instruction, that you may be wise in your latter days." Beloved active listener gains more to what is been said.

3. Hearing: It is an active term.

Hearing is piercing what someone is saying or a sound. Hearing determines the action one is about to take.

4. Retaining: It is retaining what you read or study for future reference.

You can retain what God said to you. Meditate on it day and night and renew your mind on what you read. You start to act on what you renewed in your mind.

5. Acting: When you practice the above points and began to apply them on faith.

The Scripture said, faith without action is nothing. Genuine faith is expressed in action. Without faith, it is impossible to please God. Therefore beloved, if you have faith in God, began to act on His commandments. Express your love for Him.

Time to act on what God said

Acting on what God said is the surefire way to please Him. Several chapters and passages in the Bible show how God continues to encourage His children to keep His commandments. The time to act on what God said is *Now*. Jesus said to His disciples;

"If you love Me, keep My commandments" (John 14:15). We are called and chosen to do what He said in His word. That is what the church is all about. As already said, doing what God said is the only way we can determine our love for Him. Therefore beloved, keeping the commandments of God and referencing it daily should be our everyday practice. A saying goes this way, "practice makes perfect," if you eventually fail in one aspect of obedience to God, don't get discouraged, learn a lesson from it and go back to it again, practice doing what He said to you. Let God's word rule your entire life. Discouragement is a weapon of the devil through which he pulls you from attaining to God's purposes for your life.

Discouraged life style ushers in:

- Bitterness,
- Angry,
- Regret,
- Resentment,
- Unforgiving,
- Blame of others.
- Misunderstanding.

You can avoid such discouraged lifestyle by depending and doing what God said. This is achievable through total dependence on the indwelling Holy Spirit in you. He is the only one that reveals the mind of God to you. He teaches you to follow what God said by Christ Jesus. Apostle speaking to his audience, put it this way in the book of Colossians 2:9, "For in Him dwells all the fullness of the Godhead bodily." It is important to note that Jesus is God and God is Jesus. (John 1:1). In the beginning, was the word, and the word was God, dwelling among us. Jesus is the revealed word of God. So, therefore, as you go about acting on the word of God, it is important to note that you are interacting with God Himself.

Jesus is the final word of God to humanity. He is the epitome of God in righteousness. He is the word of God who became flesh and dwelled around us. John (1:14). Just for the sake of humanity, including you and me, so that we can be free forever. He also rose from the dead for our justification. Yes, for our total emancipation from eternal damnation. Beloved of God, the question which remains to be answered precisely is, what can we do to be saved?

A lot of people has different answers to this important questions, some when posed with this question answered,

- I stay out of trouble.
- I read my bible daily.
- I help people who are in need.
- I go to the church service every Sunday or as often as I can, I serve my pastor
- I help out in the church when I am needed.
- I pray everyday as I try to help people.
- I am baptized
- My mother/Father/ brother/Sister is a preacher.

The list goes on and on. To be saved is to be delivered or set free from our past life of sin. Live a new life in Christ, which is eternal or everlasting life.

In the book of Acts of the Apostles, the jailer asked Apostle Paul after he saw the powerful move of God, what must I do to be saved? Paul answer

"Believe on the Lord Jesus Christ, and you will be saved, you and your household." Believe is the central key that moves the Lord to trust you when you confess Him as your personal Lord and savior.

Romans 10:9 says that "If you confess with your mouth the Lord Jesus and believe in your heart that God has raised Him from the dead, you will be saved." Believe is a personal choice; you can decide to believe in Him, or you can decide not to. Your belief proves who you are in the sight of God.

Look out everybody

We are living in a time the church should be looking out for the second coming of Jesus Christ. Jesus gave these signs when He was physically on the earth. He revealed to His disciples about His second coming and the end of the age (Matthew 24:5-14). God expects us to be alert and watch out for the signs given.

Jesus warned His disciples because He does not want any of His children to be taken unawares. He will come at an hour no one expects. Jesus specifically said, as it was in the days of Noah, so will it be in the coming of the son of man, people were eating and drinking, marrying and giving in marriage up until the day Noah entered the ark. Matthew 24:38

No one knows the date or time of His coming but said that all these signs must be fulfilled proceeding His coming. Almost all the signs have been fulfilled, what's more to look out for?

Are you ready? To be ready means that you have ultimately finished all that Jesus Christ required you to do while He was away in heaven. Are you engaged in doing the assignments? Or are you playing church? Are you ready even if you are taken unawares?

Jesus wants us to be ready and be busy reaching out to His people who have not heard the gospel. He does want to spend eternity in heaven with those who will believe. Are you aware of these facts?

"As I live,' says the Lord God, 'I have no pleasure in the death of the wicked, but that the wicked turn from his way and live. Turn, turn from your evil ways! For why should you die, O house of Israel?'" Ezekiel 33:11b

Jesus further said many would come in my name claiming, I am the messiah and would deceive many. You will hear of wars and rumors of war, but see to it that you are not alarmed. Such things must happen, but the end is still to come. Live for Jesus alone NOW!

Last signs

Matthew 24:14 "And this gospel of the kingdom will be preached in all the world as a witness to all the nations, and then the end will come."

Statistics show that about 7 billion people are presently living on earth. The only time we can categorically say that the gospel has reached everyone is when Jesus Christ comes. No one can claim that 7 billion has been reached with the gospel except God.

The scripture made it clear that the gospel shall be preached in all the world, then the end will come. As long as we are still alive, it is a clear evidence that message of salvation has not been preached across the world. Many have not heard the message. Therefore, beloved, as long as we are alive, God expects us to continue to share the gospel. The church is mandated to carry out this important assignment. The primary assignment which the Lord gave to the church is to reach out to the world with the gospel message of love.

All we have to do is to obey and be effective in sharing the gospel. Consequently, it calls for the churches to step outside the church walls and preach gospel in different communities. It is only through aggressive soul-winning that the church can reach out to everyone with the good news. The kingdom of God suffers from violence.

Therefore beloved when the trumpet sounds, know that the gospel has reached the whole world. God will pat on the back of everyone who has participated in taking the message of gospel to the unbelievers.

You see, sharing the gospel of our Lord Jesus Christ to those who have not heard stands as one of the final signs to be fulfilled preceding the second coming of Jesus Christ.

I believe, not everyone has heard the gospel. I do think that the church is not engaging in this mandate urgently as it supposed to be.

Specific commandments to share the good news:

Some passages in the Bible has some specific instructions about soul-winning. The book of Mark puts it this way; He (Jesus Christ) said to them, "Go into all the world and preach the gospel to every creature. He who believes and is baptized will be saved; but he who does not believe will be condemned." Mark 16:15-17. Matthew put His their way; then Jesus come to them and said,

"All authority has been given to Me in heaven and on earth. Go therefore and make disciples of all the nations, baptizing them in the name of the Father and of the Son and of the Holy Spirit, teaching them to observe all things that I have commanded you; and lo, I am with you always, even to the end of the age." Matthew 28:18-20.

Sharing the gospel is the reason that you are still alive. We are all mandated to take this mandate outside the church walls to the streets house to house and to everyone that has not heard.

You are called!
11 Corinthians 5:17-18.

"Therefore, if anyone believe in Christ, he is a new creature, Old things are passed away, Behold all things are become new. And all things are of

God who hath reconciled us to Himself by Jesus Christ and hath given to us the ministry of reconciliation."

You are saved to save. Yes, this is true; you have to help other people to have eternal life in Jesus Christ. It is seen as being selfish if you don't participate in kingdom-building. That is why Jesus Christ speaker through Apostle John said:

"In My Father's house are many mansions; if it were not so, I would have told you. I go to prepare a place for you. And if I go and prepare a place for you, I will come again and receive you to Myself; that where I am, there you may be also." John 14:2, 3.

Jesus wants you and me to win as many souls as we can. The mansions are for those who receive Jesus by faith as Lord and savior. Therefore, God commanded us (the church) to go and win souls. Winning of souls is the reason for our existence after we are saved. God prepares you and equips you for these assignments. God loves the unbelievers as much as He loves you and me; He is no respecter of persons. Heaven is still open for those who will say yes to Jesus Christ. It is not the pastor's responsibility alone to share the gospel, but everyone that has received Jesus Christ by faith as personal Lord and savior. It is your responsibility and mine as well to engage in carrying out this important mandate. Thousands of people, I believe, are yet to hear the gospel. Sharing the gospel gladdens God's heart, it gives Him joy.

My prayer remains the same as always; that the Holy Spirit will open your eyes to see the urgency needed at this time to bring the gospel message to the world.

THE FINAL NOTE

God anointed every part of our lives to be sensitive to what He said. He is much pleased if we humble ourselves and give Him our undivided attention. We are to discipline ourselves and follow His leading. The Scripture tells us that we are made in His image. (Genesis 1:27)

- Additionally, He indwells us by His Spirit, meaning that God lives inside of me.
- Wherever I am, He is there with me.
- At my job, He is there with me.
- He speaks to me. He hears my complaints.
- He knows when I am hurt.
- He knows when I am maltreated by some persons.
- He directs my ways and my thought.
- He is your light and your salvation.
- If you walk through the valley of the shadow of death, He walks with you to make sure that you are not consumed. He covers you with His blood.
- He assigned thousands of Angels to guide you.
- They are in front of you and behind you.
- They are by your side.

God speaks on your behalf to your enemies. Listen to His command issued against your enemies; "touch not my anointed ones and do my prophet no harm." Everything that God created on this planet earth obeys this commandment. We are to rule over them. You are in-charge beloved. God will bring you every blessing He has promised you if you are honest in your confession of Him.

How do you feel when you talk to your child, and he fails to give you attention, or after you spoke, he ignores you. To me, it is disrespectful and insulting. God is our father and needed our attention when He speaks to us. What He says is the way, the truth, and life. (John 14:6) You will never regret knowing Him if you do what He says.

HONESTY

Online definition of honesty says it a facet of moral character that connotes positive and virtuous attributes such as integrity, truthfulness, straightforwardness, including straightforwardness of conduct, along with the absence of lying, cheating, and theft. Honesty also involves being trustworthy, loyal, fair and sincere.

Honesty is one of the keys to being an effective and humble servant. God knows more than we know ourselves; He knows our present thought and future thoughts. He wants to call us His own. He wants to trust us.

We have to be honest with Him in all things. If you are discouraged, tell Him. If you are happy, tell him. If you are upset, tell Him. If you are disappointed in something, tell Him. If someone accuses you of something you did, or did not, tell Him. If it is something you did Tell Him. If you make certain decision that has put you into trouble tell Him. If you want to make a decision of something, tell him so He can lead you to the right part. If you are going out with a friend, tell Him. Beloved, form a habit of letting God know everything about you. If you tell lies, tell Him. If you want to travel, tell Him. Even when you want to make a decision about the kind of clothes that you want to put on before you leave for work for the day, tell him.

Remember He already knows everything that you are about to say. Be honest in your relationship with Him.

THE HOLY SPIRIT
His qualities

The Holy Spirit is the key to achieving a good and unadulterated relationship with Jesus.

Holy Spirit is God living inside of you.

He reveals the mind of God.

The Holy Spirit helps you live a Christian lifestyle.

He directs your everyday living and speaks to you consistently.

He is the power of God operating in you.

He confirms you as a child of God and gives you the assurance of your salvation.

He convicts you of sins. He forgives you if you confess and repent from your sins.

He reveals the Cross of Jesus Christ.

He tells you the truth of the word of God.

He speaks through you to the unbelievers.

He confirms the word of God you spoke over a situation to bring the desired result.

He enables you to speak and write about Him.

He anoints you to write a book just as He empowered me to write this volume.

He is a person.

He is kind and gentle.

He has feelings.

He enjoys your recognition of Him.

He answers you when you call on Him.

He reveals God's purpose for your life.

He will guide your decision and make sure that it is fulfilled to the glory of His name.

One cannot successfully live a Christian life without the leading of the Holy Spirit.

You are to constantly recognize the presence of the Holy Spirit in your life, and as you do begin to make Him your best friend, your trusted partner in the ministry. He illuminates your heart with His presence. Holy Spirit is also the power of God in creation. He constantly ministers to you what God said. He comes to indwell you immediately when you give your life over to God by receiving Jesus Christ as your Lord and personal savior.

On a hill far away stood an old rugged cross
The emblem of suffering and shame
And I love that old cross where the dearest and best
for a world of lost sinners was slayed.
So I'll cherish the old rugged cross
Till my trophies, at last, I lay down
I will cling to the old rugged cross and exchange it someday for a crown

In that old rugged cross, stained with blood so divine a wonderful beauty I see for 't' was on that old cross Jesus suffered and died. George Bernard (1873-1958).

Perhaps this is one of the songs that remind us of the incident at the cross of Calvary. It has been a song for heaven-bound Christians. The song reminds us of the reality of meeting with Jesus Christ when our time is up in this side of eternity.

It focuses on the suffering that Jesus went through in order to secure our eternity in heaven. He shed His blood for humanity so he who believes and confesses Him as Lord and personal Savior will have eternal life.

The cross stands as a place of suffering. It is also a place of deliverance. Every believer of Jesus has victory over Satan. As we still live here on the earth, our life circles around the cross until we exchange it for a crown.

If you want to wear the crown of victory, the preparation starts now. Paul said, "Which thing we're given to me now I count it lost for the sake of Christ?"

Whatever thing you are counting great in your life maybe your title, education, position, wealth, family, or whatever it is if you want to be sure that you make it to the end, as Paul said count them as nothing, then focus on Jesus Christ. Hebrew 12:2 encourages us to focus unto Jesus, the author, and finisher of our faith, trusting Him and doing what He asked us to do.

Paul counted everything he has achieved in life as nothing. He focused on Jesus alone to fulfill his ministry. As a Christian and a believer of Jesus Christ, your ultimate or immediate goal should be to do what God said.

My Arch Bishop, LeRoy Bailey Jr. The senior Pastor of the First Cathedral church in Bloomfield once said, "As long as I have Christ in me, every other thing does not matter." The relationship he has with Jesus Christ is what matters most in his life. He can still anchor to Jesus with or without music or choir, or any other means of worship people hold on to. This is what I believe to be legitimate faith in Jesus Christ. Jesus Christ alone period. Every other thing follows. I pray that God will bless and keep you until we meet in heaven and part no more.

Sincerely.
Rev. Dr. Chris Okeke. 02-14-20.

Printed in the United States
By Bookmasters